Emile Erckmann, Alexandre Chatrian

The blockade of Phalsburg

An episode of the end of the empire

Emile Erckmann, Alexandre Chatrian

The blockade of Phalsburg
An episode of the end of the empire

ISBN/EAN: 9783337235079

Printed in Europe, USA, Canada, Australia, Japan

Cover: Foto ©ninafisch / pixelio.de

More available books at **www.hansebooks.com**

EVERYTHING WAS DEAD.

NATIONAL NOVELS

THE

BLOCKADE OF PHALSBURG

An Episode of the End of the Empire

TRANSLATED FROM THE FRENCH OF

ERCKMANN-CHATRIAN

NEW YORK
CHARLES SCRIBNER'S SONS
1889

COPYRIGHT, 1871, BY
CHARLES SCRIBNER & CO.

COPYRIGHT, 1889, BY
CHARLES SCRIBNER'S SONS

TROW'S
PRINTING AND BOOKBINDING COMPANY,
NEW YORK.

INTRODUCTORY NOTE.

"The Blockade of Phalsburg" contains one of the happiest portraits in the Erckmann-Chatrian gallery—that of the Jew Moses who tells the story and who is always in character, however great the patriotic or romantic temptation to idealize him, and whose character is nevertheless portrayed with an almost affectionate appreciation of the sterling qualities underlying its somewhat usurious exterior. The time is 1814, during the invasion of France by the allies after the disastrous battle of Leipsic and the campaign described in "The Conscript." The dwellers in Phalsburg—a little walled town of two or three thousand inhabitants in Lorraine—defend themselves with great intrepidity and determination during the siege which lasts until the capitulation of Paris. The daily life of the citizens and garrison, the various incidents of the blockade, the bombardment by night, the scarcity of food, the occasional sortie for foraging, all pass before the reader depicted with the authors' customary fidelity and life-likeness, and form as perfect a picture of a siege as "The Conscript" does of a campaign.

CONTENTS.

CHAP.		PAGE
I.	Father Moses and his Family	5
II.	Father Moses' Speculation	22
III.	A Circumcision Feast	33
IV.	Father Moses compelled to bear Arms	44
V.	Father Moses receives Welcome News	61
VI.	A Disagreeable Guest	72
VII.	Sergeant Trubert in a New Light	85
VIII.	Father Moses' First Encounter	93
IX.	Approach of the Enemy	108
X.	An Engagement with the Cossacks	120
XI.	Father Moses Returns in Triumph	134
XII.	The Enemy Repulsed	145
XIII.	A Deserter Captured	166
XIV.	Burguet's Visit to the Deserter	190
XV.	Trial of the Deserter	202
XVI.	A Sortie of the Garrison	224
XVII.	Famine and Fever	251
XVIII.	Death of Little David	262
XIX.	The Passover	276
XX.	Peace	288
XXI.		307

THE BLOCKADE:

AN EPISODE OF THE END OF THE EMPIRE.

I.

FATHER MOSES AND HIS FAMILY.

Since you wish to know about the blockade of Phalsburg in 1814, I will tell you all about it, said father Moses of the Jews' street.

I lived then in the little house on the corner, at the right of the market. My business was selling iron by the pound, under the arch below, and I lived above with my wife Sorlé (Sarah) and my little Sâfel, the child of my old age.

My two other boys, Itzig and Frômel, had gone to America, and my daughter Zeffin was married to Baruch, the leather-dealer, at Saverne.

Besides my iron business, I traded in old shoes,

old linen, and all the articles of old clothing which conscripts sell on reaching the depot, where they receive their military outfit. Travelling pedlers bought the old linen of me for paper-rags, and the other things I sold to the country people.

This was a profitable business, because thousands of conscripts passed through Phalsburg from week to week, and from month to month. They were measured at once at the mayoralty, clothed, and filed off to Mayence, Strasburg, or wherever it might be.

This lasted a long time; but at length people were tired of war, especially after the Russian campaign and the great recruiting of 1813.

You may well suppose, Fritz, that I did not wait till this time before sending my two boys beyond the reach of the recruiting officers' clutches. They were boys who did not lack sense. At twelve years old their heads were clear enough, and rather than go and fight for the King of Prussia, they would see themselves safe at the ends of the earth.

At evening, when we sat at supper around the lamp with its seven burners, their mother would sometimes cover her face and say:

"My poor children! My poor children! When

I think that the time is near when you will go in the midst of musket and bayonet fire—in the midst of thunder and lightning!—oh, how dreadful'"

And I saw them turn pale. I smiled at myself and thought: "You are no fools. You will hold on to your life. That is right!"

If I had had children capable of becoming soldiers, I should have died of grief. I should have said, "These are not of my race!"

But the boys grew stronger and handsomer. When Itzig was fifteen he was doing a good business. He bought cattle in the villages on his own account, and sold them at a profit to butcher Borich at Mittelbronn; and Frômel was not behind him, for he made the best bargains of the old merchandise, which we had heaped in three barracks under the market.

I should have liked well to keep the boys with me. It was my delight to see them with my little Säfel—the curly head and eyes bright as a squirrel's—yes, it was my joy! Often I clasped them in my arms without a word, and even they wondered at it; I frightened them; but dreadful thoughts passed through my mind after 1812. I knew that whenever the Emperor had returned to Paris, he had demanded four hundred millions of francs and two or three hundred thousand men, and I said to myself:

"This time, everybody must go, even children of seventeen and eighteen!"

As the tidings grew worse and worse, I said to them one evening:

"Listen! you both understand trading, and what you do not yet know you can learn. Now, if you wait a few months, you will be on the conscription list, and be like all the rest; they will take you to the square and show you how to load a gun, and then you will go away, and I never shall hear of you again!"

Sorlé sighed, and we all sighed together. Then, after a moment, I continued:

"But if you set out at once for America, by the way of Havre, you will reach it safe and sound; you will do business there as well as here; you will make money, you will marry, you will increase according to the Lord's promise, and you will send me back money, according to God's commandment, 'Honor thy father and thy mother's. I will bless you as Isaac blessed Jacob, and you will have a long life. Choose!"

They at once chose to go to America, and I went with them myself as far as Sorreburg. Each of them had made twenty louis in his own business, so that I needed to give them nothing but my blessing.

And what I said to them has come to pass; they are both living, they have numerous children, who are my descendants, and when I want anything they send it to me.

Itzig and Frömel being gone, I had only Säfel left, my Benjamin, dearer even, if possible, than the others. And then, too, I had my daughter Zeffen, married at Saverne to a good respectable man, Baruch; she was the oldest, and had already given me a grandson named David, according to the Lord's will that the dead should be replaced in his own family, and David was the name of Baruch's grandfather. The one expected was to be called after my father, Esdras.

You see, Fritz, how I was situated before the blockade of Phalsburg, in 1814. Everything had gone well up to that time, but for six weeks everything had gone wrong in town and country. We had the typhus; thousands of wounded soldiers surrounded the houses; the ground had lacked laborers for the last two years, and everything was dear—bread, meat, and drink. The people of Alsace and Lorraine did not come to market; our stores of merchandise did not sell; and when merchandise does not sell, it might as well be sand or stones; we are poor in the midst of abundance. Famine comes from every quarter.

Ah, well! in spite of it all, the Lord had a great blessing in store for me, for just at this time, early in November, came the news that a second son was born to Zeffen, and that he was in fine health. I was so glad that I set out at once for Saverne.

You must know, Fritz, that if I was very glad, it was not only on account of the birth of a grandson, but also because my son-in-law would not be obliged to leave home, if the child lived. Baruch had always been fortunate; at the moment when the Emperor had made the Senate vote that unmarried men must go, he had just married Zeffen; and when the Senate voted that married men without children must go, he had his first child. Now, after the bad news, it was voted that married men with only one child should go, all the same, and Baruch had two.

At that time it was a fortunate thing to have quantities of children, to keep you from being massacred; no greater blessing could be desired! This is why I took my cane at once, to go and find out whether the child were sound and healthy, and whether it would save its father.

But for long years to come, if God spares my life, I shall remember that day, and what I met upon my way.

Imagine the road-side blocked, as it were, with carts filled with the sick and wounded, forming a line all the way from Quatre-Vents to Saverne.

The peasants who, in Alsace, were required to transport these poor creatures, had unharnessed their horses and escaped in the night, abandoning their carts; the hoar-frost had passed over them; there was not motion or sign of life—all dead, as it were one long cemetery! Thousands of ravens covered the sky like a cloud; there was nothing to be seen but wings moving in the air, nothing to be heard but one murmur of innumerable cries. I would not have believed that heaven and earth could produce so many ravens. They flew down to the very carts; but the moment a living man approached, all these creatures rose and flew away to the forest of La Bonne-Fontaine, or the ruins of the old convent of Dann.

As for myself, I lengthened my steps, feeling that I must not stop, that the typhus was marching at my heels.

Happily the winter sets in early at Phalsburg. A cold wind blew from the Schneeberg, and these strong draughts of mountain air disperse all maladies, even, it is said, the Black Plague itself.

What I have now told you is about the retreat from Leipsic, in the beginning of November.

When I reached Saverne, the city was crowded with troops, artillery, infantry, and cavalry, pell-mell.

I remember that, in the principal street, the windows of an inn were open, and a long table with its white cloth was seen, all laid, within. All the guard of honor stopped there. These were young men of rich families, who had money in spite of their tattered uniforms. The moment they saw this table in passing, they leaped from their horses and rushed into the hall. But the innkeeper, Hannès, made them pay five francs in advance, and just as the poor things began to eat, a servant ran in, crying out, "The Prussians! the Prussians!" They sprang up at once and mounted their horses like madmen, without once looking back, and in this way Hannès sold his dinner more than twenty times.

I have often thought since that such scoundrels

deserve hanging; yes, this way of making money is not lawful business. It disgusted me.

But if I should describe the rest—the faces of the sick, the way in which they lay, the groans they uttered, and, above all, the tears of those who tried in vain to go on—if I should tell you this, it would be still worse, it would be too much. I saw, on the slope of the old tan-house bridge, a little guardsman of seventeen or eighteen years, stretched out, with his face flat upon the stones. I have never forgotten that boy; he raised himself from time to time, and showed his hand as black as soot: he had a ball in the back, and his hand was half gone. The poor fellow had doubtless fallen from a cart. Nobody dared to help him because they heard it said, "He has the typhus! he has the typhus." Oh, what misery! It is too dreadful to think of!

Now, Fritz, I must tell you another thing about that day, and that is how I saw Marshal Victor.

It was late when I started from Phalsburg, and it was dark when, on going up the principal street of Saverne, I saw all the windows of the Hotel du Soleil illuminated from top to bottom. Two sentinels walked to and fro under the arch, officers in full uniform went in and out, magnificent horses were fastened to rings all along the walls; and, within the court, the lamps of a calash shone like two stars.

The sentinels kept the street clear, but I must pass, because Baruch dwelt further on. I was going through the crowd, in front of the hotel, and the first sentinel was calling out to me, "Back! back!" when an officer of hussars, a short, stout man, with great red whiskers, came out of the arch, and as he met me, exclaimed,

"Ah! is it you, Moses! I am glad to see you!"

He shook hands with me.

I opened my eyes with amazement, as was natural: a superior officer shaking hands with a plain citizen is not an every-day occurrence. I looked at him in astonishment, and recognized Commandant Zimmer.

Thirty years before we had been at Father Genaudet's school, and we had scoured the city, the moats, and the glacis together, as children. But since then Zimmer had been a good many times in Phalsburg, without remembering his old comrade, Samuel Moses.

"Ho!" said he, smiling, and taking me by the arm "come, I must present you to the marshal."

And, in spite of myself, before I had said a

word, I went in under the arch, into a large room where two long tables, loaded with lights and bottles, were laid for the staff-officers.

A number of superior officers, generals, colonels, commanders of hussars, of dragoons and of chasseurs, in plumed hats, in helmets, in red shakos, their chins in their huge cravats, their swords dragging, were walking silently back and forth, or talking with each other, while they waited to be called to table.

It was difficult to pass through the crowd, but Zimmer kept hold of my arm, and led me to the end of the room, to a little lighted door.

We entered a high room, with two windows opening upon the gardens.

The marshal was there, standing, his head uncovered; his back was toward us, and he was dictating orders which two staff-officers were writing.

This was all which I noticed at the moment, in my confusion.

Just after we entered, the marshal turned; I saw that he had the good face of an old Lorraine peasant. He was a tall, powerful man, with a grayish head; he was about fifty years old, and very heavy for his age.

"Marshal, here's our man!" said Zimmer. "He is one of my old schoolmates, Samuel Moses, a first-rate fellow, who has been traversing the country these thirty years, and knows every village in Alsace and Lorraine."

The marshal looked at me a few steps off. I held my hat in my hand in great fear. After looking at me a couple of seconds, he took the paper which one of the secretaries handed him, read and signed it, then turned back to me:

"Well, my good man," said he, "what do they say about the last campaign? What do the people in your village think about it?"

On hearing him call me "my good man," I took courage, and answered "that the typhus had made bad work, but the people were not disheartened, because they knew that the Emperor with his army was at hand."

And when he said abruptly: "Yes! But will they defend themselves?" I answered: "The Alsatians and the Lorraines are people who will defend themselves till death, because they love their Emperor, and they would all be willing to die for him!"

I said that by way of prudence; but he could plainly see in my face that I was no fighting man, for he smiled good-humoredly, and said: "That will do, Commandant, that is enough!"

The secretaries had kept on writing. Zimmer made a sign to me and we went out together. When we were outside he called out:

"Good-by, Moses, good-by!"

The sentinels let me pass, and still trembling, I continued my journey.

I was soon knocking at the little door of Baruch's house at the end of the lane where the cardinal's old stables were.

It was pitch dark.

What a joy it was, Fritz, after having seen all these terrible things, to come to the place where those I loved were resting! How softly my heart beat, and how I pitied all that power and glory which made so many people miserable!

After a moment I heard my son-in-law enter the passage and open the door. Baruch and Zeffen had long since ceased expecting me.

"Is it you, my father?" asked Baruch.

"Yes, my son, it is I. I am late. I have been hindered."

"Come!" said he.

And we entered the little passage, and then

into the chamber where Zeffen, my daughter, lay pale and happy, upon her bed.

She had recognized my voice. As for me, my heart beat with joy; I could not speak; and I embraced my daughter, while I looked around to find the little one. Zeffen held it in her arms under the coverlet.

"There he is!" she said.

Then she showed him to me in his swaddling-clothes. I saw at once that he was plump and healthy, with his little hands closed tight, and I exclaimed:

"Baruch, this is Esdras, my father! Let him be welcome!"

I wanted to see him without his clothes, so I undressed him. It was warm in the little room from the lamp with seven burners. Tremblingly I undressed him; he did not cry, and my daughter's white hands assisted me:

"Wait, my father, wait!" said she.

My son-in-law looked on behind me. We all had tears in our eyes.

At last I had him all undressed; he was rosy, and his large head tossed about, sleeping the sleep of centuries. Then I lifted him above my head;

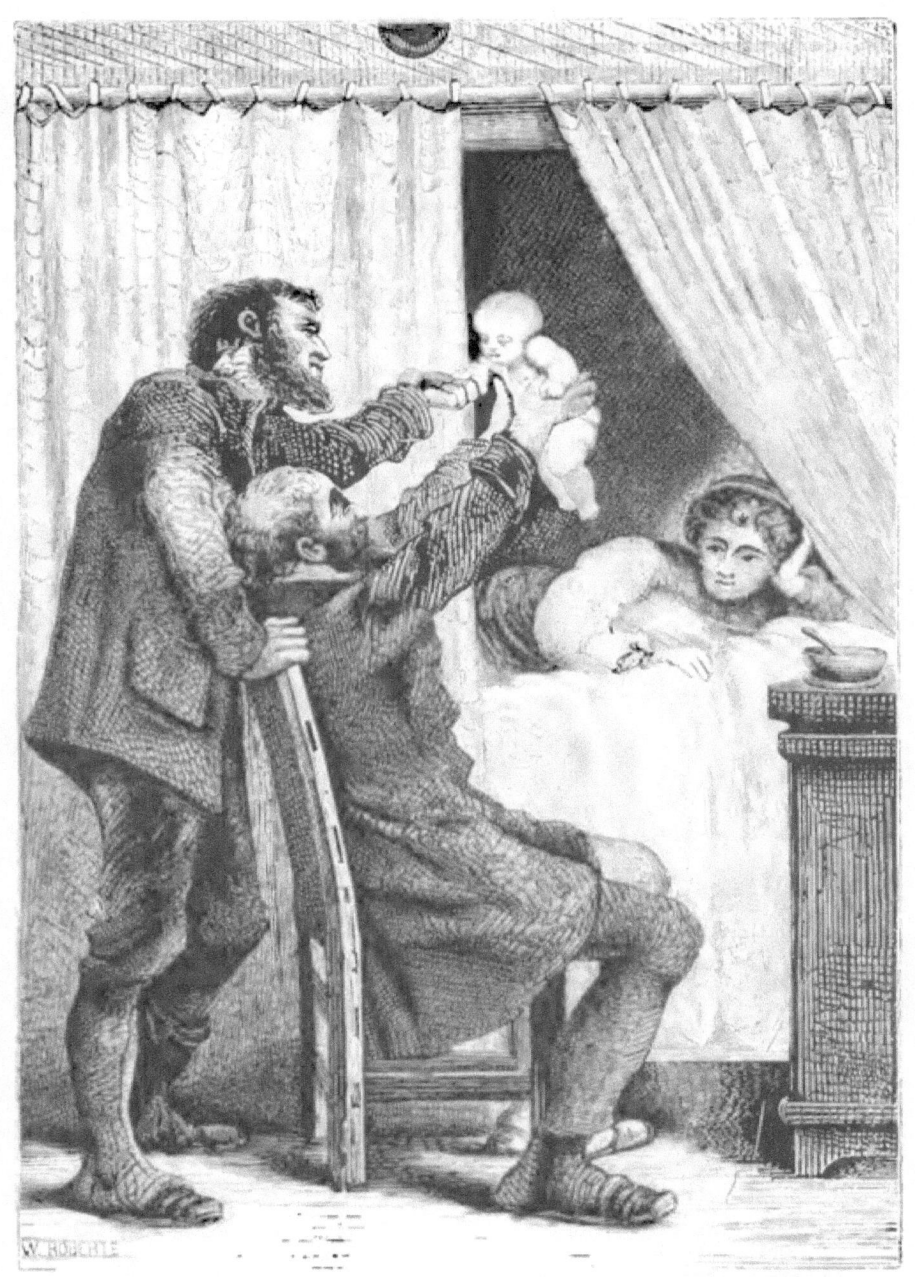

"HE WILL BE THE JOY OF OUR OLD AGE."

I looked at his round thighs all in creases, at his little drawn-up feet, his broad chest and plump back, and I wanted to dance like David before the ark; I wanted to chant: "Praise the Lord! Praise him ye servants of the Lord! Praise the name of the Lord! Blessed be the name of the Lord from this time forth and forever more! From the rising of the sun, unto the going down of the same, the Lord's name is to be praised! The Lord is high above all nations, and his glory above the heavens! Who is like unto the Lord our God, who raiseth up the poor out of the dust, who maketh the barren woman to keep house, and to be a joyful mother of children? Praise ye the Lord!"

Yes, I felt like chanting this, but all that I could say was: He is a fine, perfect child! He is going to live! He will be the blessing of our race and the joy of our old age!"

And I blessed them all.

Then giving him back to his mother to be covered, I went to embrace the other who was sound asleep in his cradle.

We remained there together a long time, to see each other, in this joy. Without, horses were passing, soldiers shouting, carriages rolling by. Here all was quiet: the mother nursed her infant.

Ah! Fritz, I am an old man now, and these far-off things are always before me, as at the first; my heart always beats in recalling them, and I thank God for His great goodness,—I thank Him He has loaded me with years, he has permitted me to see the third generation, and I am not weary of life; I should like to live on and see the fourth and the fifth—His will be done!

I should have liked to tell them of what had just happened to me at the Hotel du Soleil, but everything was insignificant in comparison with my joy; only after I had left the chamber, while I was taking a mouthful of bread and drinking a glass of wine in the side hall so as to let Zeffen sleep, I related the adventure to Baruch, who was greatly surprised.

"Listen, my son," said I, "this man asked me if we want to defend ourselves. That shows that the allies are following our armies, that they are marching by hundreds of thousands, and that they cannot be hindered from entering France. So you see that, in the midst of our joy, there is danger of terrible evils; you see that all the harm which we have been doing to others for these last ten years may return upon us. I fear so. God grant that I may be mistaken!"

After this we went to bed. It was eleven o'clock, and the tumult without still continued.

II.

FATHER MOSES' SPECULATION.

Early the next morning, after breakfast, I took my cane to return to Phalsburg. Zeffen and Baruch wanted to keep me longer, but I said:

"You do not think of your mother, who is expecting me. She does not keep still a minute; she keeps going up stairs and down, and looking out of the window. No, I must go. Sorlé must not be uneasy while we are comfortable."

Zeffen said no more, and filled my pockets with apples and nuts for her brother Sâfel. I embraced them again, the little ones and the big; then Baruch led me far back of the gardens, to the place where the roads to Schlittenbach and Lutzelburg divide.

The troops had all left, only stragglers and the sick remaining. But we could still see the line of carts in the distance, on the hill, and bands of day-laborers who had been set to work digging graves back of the road.

The very thought of passing that way disturbed me. I shook hands with Baruch at this fork of the road, promising to come again with grandmother to the circumcision, and then took the valley road, which follows the Zorn through the woods.

This path was full of dead leaves, and for two hours I walked on thinking at times of the Hotel du Soleil, of Zimmer, of Marshal Victor, whom I seemed to see again, with his tall figure, his square shoulders, his gray head, and coat covered with embroidery. Sometimes I pictured to myself Zeffen's chamber, the little babe and its mother; then the war which threatened us—that mass of enemies advancing from every side!

Several times I stopped in the midst of these valleys sloping into each other as far as the eye can reach, all covered with firs, oaks and beeches, and I said to myself:

"Who knows? Perhaps the Prussians, Austrians and Russians will soon pass along here!"

But there was comfort in this thought; "Moses, your two boys, Itzig and Frömel, are in America far from the reach of cannon; they are there with their packs on their shoulders, going from village to village without danger. And your daughter Zeffen, too, may sleep in quiet; Baruch has two fine children, and will have another every year while the war lasts. He will sell leather to make bags and shoes for those who have to go, but, for his part, he will stay at home."

I smiled as I thought that I was too old to be conscripted, that I was a gray-head, and the conscriptors could have none of us. Yes; I smiled as I saw that I had acted very wisely in everything, and that the Lord had, as it were, cleared my path.

It is a great satisfaction, Fritz, to see that everything is working to our advantage.

In the midst of these thoughts I came quietly to Lutzelburg, and I went to Brestel's at the Swan Hotel to take a cup of coffee.

There I found Bernard, the soap merchant, whom you do not know—a little man, bald to the very nape of the neck, with great wens on his head—and Donadieu, the Harberg forest-keeper. One had laid his dosser and the other his gun against the wall, and they were emptying a bottle of wine between them. Brestel was helping.

"Ha! it is Moses," exclaimed Bernard. "Where the devil dost thou come from, so early in the morning!"

Christians in those days were in the habit of *thou*-ing the Jews—even the old men. I answered that I had come from Saverne, by the valley.

"Ah! thou hast seen the wounded," said the keeper. "What thinkest thou of that, Moses!"

"I have seen them," I replied sadly, "I saw them last evening. It is dreadful!"

"Yes, it is; everybody has gone up there to-day, because old Gredal of Quatre-Vents found her nephew under a cart—Joseph Bertha, the little lame watchmaker who worked last year with father Goulden; so the people from Dagsberg, Houpe, and Garburg, expect to find their brothers, or sons, or cousins in the heap."

He shrugged his shoulders compassionately.

"These things are dreadful," said Brestel, "but they must come. There has been no business these two years; I have back here, in my court, three thousand pounds' worth of planks and timber. That would formerly have lasted me for six weeks or two months; but now it is all rotting on the spot; nobody wants it on the Sarre, nobody wants it in Alsace, nobody orders anything or buys anything. It is just so with the hotel. Nobody has a sous; everybody stays at home, thankful if they have potatoes to eat and cold water to drink. Mean while my wine and beer turn sour in the cellar, and are covered with mildew. And all that does not keep off the duties; you must pay, or the officer will be upon you."

"Yes," cried Bernard, "it is the same thing everywhere. But what is it to the Emperor whether planks and soap sell or not, provided the contributions come in and the conscripts arrive?"

Donadieu perceived that his comrade had taken a glass too much; he rose, put back his gun into his shoulder-belt, and went out, calling to us.

"Good-by to you all, good-by! We will talk about this another time."

A few minutes afterward, I paid for my cup of coffee, and followed his example.

I had the same thoughts as Brestel and Bernard; I saw that my trade in iron and old clothes was at an end; and as I went up the Barracks' hill I thought, "Try to find something else, Moses. Everything is at a stand-still. But one cannot use up his money to the last farthing. I must turn to something else—I must find an article which is always salable. But what is always salable? Every trade has its day, and then it comes to an end."

While thus meditating, I passed the Barracks of the Bois-de-Chênes. I was on the plateau from which I could see the glacis, the line of ramparts, and the bastions, when the firing of a cannon gave notice that the marshal was leaving the place. At the same time I saw at the left, in the direction of Mittelbronn, the line of sabres flashing like lightning in the distance among the poplars of the highway. The trees were leafless, and I could see, too, the carriage and postilions passing like the wind through the plumes and caps.

The cannon pealed, second after second; the mountains gave back peal after peal, from the very depths of their valleys; and as for myself, I was quite carried away by the thought of having seen this man the day before; it seemed like a dream.

Then, about ten o'clock, I passed the bridge of the French gate. The last cannon sounded upon the bastion of the powder-house; the crowd of men, women and children descended the ramparts, as if it were a festival; they knew nothing, thought of nothing, while cries of "Vive l'Empereur!" rose in every street.

I passed through the crowd, well pleased at bringing good news to my wife; and I was saying to myself beforehand, "The little one is doing well, Sorlé!" when, at the corner of the market, I saw her at our door. I raised my cane at once, and smiled, as much as to say "Baruch is safe—we may laugh!"

She understood me, and went in at once; but I overtook her on the stairs, and embraced her, saying:

"It is a good, hearty little fellow—there! Such a baby—so round and rosy! And Zeffen is doing well. Baruch wished me to embrace you for him. But where is Säfel?"

"Under the market, selling."

"Ah, good!"

We went into our room. I sat down and began to praise Zeffen's baby. Sorlé listened with delight, looking at me with her great black eyes, and wiping my forehead, for I had walked fast, and could hardly breathe.

And then, all of a sudden, our Säfel came in. I had not time to turn my head before he was on my knees, with his hands in my pockets. The child knew that his sister Zeffen never forgot him; and Sorlé, too, liked to bite an apple.

You see, Fritz, when I think of these things, everything comes back to me; I could talk to you about it forever.

It was Friday, the day before the Sabbath;

the *Schabbés-Goïé** was to come in the afternoon. While we were still alone at dinner, and I related for the fifth and sixth time how Zimmer had recognized me, how he had taken me into the presence of the Duke of Bellune, my wife told me that the marshal had made the tour of our ramparts on horseback, with his staff-officers; that he had examined the advanced works, the bastions, the glacis, and that he had said, as he went down the college street, that the place would hold out for eighteen days, and that it must be fortified immediately.

I remembered at once that he had asked me if we wished to defend ourselves, and I exclaimed: "He is sure that the enemy is coming; since he is going to put cannon upon the ramparts, it is because there will be need of them. It is not nattural to make preparations which are not to be used. And, if the allies come, the gates will be shut. What will become of us without our business? The country people can neither go in nor out, and what will become of us?"

Then Sorlé showed her good sense, for she said:

"I have already thought about this, Moses; it

---

* Woman, not Israelite, who on Saturday performs in a Jewish household the labors forbidden by the law of Moses is only the peasants who buy iron, old shoes, and our other things. We must undertake a city business for all classes—a business which will oblige citizens, soldiers and workmen to buy of us. That is what we must do."

I looked at her in surprise. Sâfel, with his elbow on the table, was also listening.

"It is all very well, Sorlé," I replied, "but what business is there which will oblige citizens, soldiers, everybody to buy of us—what business is there?"

"Listen," said she; "if the gates are shut and the country people cannot enter, there will be no eggs, butter, fish, or anything in the market. People will have to live on salt meats and dried vegetables, flour, and all kinds of preserved articles. Those who have bought up these can sell them at their own price; they will grow rich."

As I listened I was struck with astonishment.

"Ah, Sorlé! Sorlé!" I exclaimed, "for thirty years you have been my comfort. Yes, you have crowned me with all sorts of blessings, and I have said a hundred times, 'A good wife is a diamond of pure water, and without flaw. A good wife is a rich treasure for her husband.' I have repeated it a hundred times. But now I know still better what you are worth, and esteem you still more highly."

The more I thought of it, the more I perceived the wisdom of this advice. At length I said:

"Sorlé, meat and flour, and everything which can be kept, are already in the storehouses, and the soldiers will not need such things for a long time, because their officers will have provided them. But what will be wanted is brandy, which men must have to massacre and exterminate each other in war, and brandy we will buy! We will have plenty of it in our cellar, we will sell it, and nobody else will have it. That is my idea!"

"It is a good idea, Moses!" said she; "your reasons are good; I approve of them."

"Then I will write," said I, "and we will invest everything in spirits of wine. We will add water ourselves, in proportion as people wish to pay for it. In this way the freight will be less than if it were brandy, for we shall not have to pay for the transportation of the water, which we have here."

"That is well, Moses," she said.

And so we agreed.

Then I said to Sâfel:

"You must not speak of this to any one."

She answered for him:

"There's no need of telling him that, Moses. Sâfel knows very well that this is between ourselves, and that our well-being depends upon it."

The child for a long time resented my words: "You must not speak of this to any one." He was already full of good sense, and said to himself:

"So my father thinks I am an idiot."

This thought humiliated him. Some years afterward he told me of it, and I perceived that I had been wrong.

Everybody has his notions. Children should not be humiliated in theirs, but rather upheld by their parents.

III.

A CIRCUMCISION FEAST.

So I wrote to Pézenas. This is a southern city, rich in wools, wines, and brandies. The price of brandies at Pézenas controls that of all Europe. A trading man ought to know that, and I knew it, because I had always liked to read the list of prices in the newspapers. I sent to M. Quataya, at Pézenas, for a dozen pipes of spirits of wine. I calculated that, after paying the freight, a pipe would cost me a thousand francs, delivered in my cellar.

As I had sold no iron for a year, I disposed of my merchandise without asking anything for it; the payment of the twelve thousand francs did not trouble me. Only, Fritz, those twelve thousand francs were half my fortune, and you may suppose that it required some courage to risk in one venture the gains of fifteen years.

As soon as my letter was gone, I wished I could

bring it back, but it was too late. I kept a good face before my wife, and said, "It will all do well! We shall gain double, triple, etc."

She, too, kept a good face, but we both had misgivings; and during the six weeks necessary for the receipt of the acknowledgment and acceptance of my order, and the arrival of the spirits of wine, every night I lay awake, thinking, "Moses, you have lost everything! You are ruined from top to toe!"

The cold sweat would cover my body. Still, if any one had come to me and said, "Be easy, Moses, I will relieve you of this business," I should have refused, because my hope of gain was as great as my fear of loss. And by this you may know who are the true merchants, the true generals, and all who accomplish anything. Others are but machines for selling tobacco, or filling glasses, or firing guns.

It all comes to the same thing. One man's glory is as great as another's. This is why, when we speak of Austerlitz, Jena, or Wagram, it is not a question of Jean Claude or Jean Nicholas, but of Napoleon alone; he alone risked everything, the others risked only being killed.

I do not say this to compare myself with Napoleon, but the buying of these twelve pipes of spirits of wine was my battle of Austerlitz.

And when I think that, on reaching Paris, Napoleon had demanded four hundred and forty millions of money, and *six hundred thousand men!* and that then everybody, understanding that we were threatened with an invasion, undertook to sell and to make money at any cost, while I bought, unhampered by the example of others, —when I think of this, I am proud of it still and congratulate myself.

It was in the midst of these disquietudes that the day for the circumcision of little Esdras arrived. My daughter Zeffen had recovered, and Baruch had written to us not to trouble ourselves, for they would come to Phalsburg.

My wife then hastened to prepare the meats and cakes for the festival: the *bie-kougel*, the *haman*, and the *schlachmoness*, which are great delicacies.

On my part, I had tested my best wine on the old Rabbi Heymann, and I had invited my friends, Leiser of Mittelbronn and his wife Boúné, Senterlé Hirsch, and Professor Burguet. Burguet was not a Jew, but he was worthy of being one on account of his genius and extraordinary talents.

When a speech was wanted in the Emperor's progress, Burguet made it; when songs were needed for a national festival, Burguet composed them between two sips of beer; when a young candidate for law or medicine was perplexed in writing his thesis, he went to Burguet, who wrote it for him, whether in French or in Latin; when fathers and mothers were to be moved to tears at the distribution of school prizes, Burguet was the man to do it; he would take a blank sheet of paper, and read them a discourse on the spot, such as nobody else could have written in ten years; when a petition was to be made to the Emperor or prefect, Burguet was the first man thought of; and when Burguet took the trouble to defend a deserter before the court-martial at the mayoralty, the deserter, instead of being shot on the bastion of the barracks, was pardoned.

After all this, Burguet would return and take his part in piquet with the little Jew, Solomon, at which he always lost; and people troubled themselves no more about him.

I have often thought that Burguet must have greatly despised those to whom he took off his hat. Yes, to see the fellows putting on important airs because they were rural guard or secretary of the mayoralty, must have made a man like him laugh in his sleeve. But he never told me so; he knew the ways of the world too well.

He was an old constitutional priest, a tall man, with a noble figure and very fine voice: the very tones of it would move you in spite of yourself. Unfortunately, he did not take care of his own interests; he was at the mercy of the first comer. How many times I have said to him:

"Burguet, in heaven's name, don't get mixed up with thieves! Burguet, don't let yourself be robbed by simpletons! Trust me about your college expenses. When anybody comes to impose upon you I will be on the spot; I will pay the bills and hand you the account.

But he did not think of the future, and lived very carelessly.

I had thus invited all my old friends for the morning of the twenty-fourth of November, and they all came to the festival.

The father and mother, with the little infant, and its godfather and godmother, came early, in a large carriage. By eleven the ceremony had taken place in our synagogue, and we all, in great joy and satisfaction, for the child had not uttered a cry, returned together to my house, which had been made ready beforehand—the large table on the first floor, the meats in their pewter dishes, the fruits in their baskets—and we had begun in great glee to celebrate the happy day.

The old Rabbi Heymann, Leiser, and Burguet sat at my right, my little Säfel, Hirsch, and Baruch at my left, and the women Sorlé, Zeffen, Jételé, and Boûné, facing us on the other side, according to the command of the Lord, that men and women should be separate at festivities.

Burguet, with his white cravat, his handsome maroon coat and his ruffled shirt, did me honor. He made a speech, raising his voice and making fine gestures like a great orator—telling of the ancient customs of our nation, of our religious ceremonies, of *Paeçach* (the feast of Passover), of *Roschhaschannah* (the New Year), of *Kippour* (the day of expiation), like a true *Ied* (Jew), thinking our religion very beautiful and glorifying the genius of Moses.

He knew the *Lochene Köidech* (Chaldaic) as well as a *bal-kebolé* (cabalistic doctor).

The Saverne people turned to their neighbors and asked in a whisper:

"Pray, who is this man who speaks with an

thority, and says such fine things? Is he a rabbi? Is he a *schamess* (Jewish beadle)? or is he the *parness* (civil head) of your community?"

And when they learned he was not one of us, they were astonished. The old Rabbi Heymann alone was able to answer him, and they agreed on all points, like learned men talking on familiar subjects and conscious of their own learning.

Behind us, on its grandmother's bed, inside of the curtains, slept our little Esdras, with his sweet face and little clenched hands—slept so soundly, that neither our shouts of laughter, nor the talking, nor the sound of the glasses could wake him. Sometimes one, sometimes another, went to look at him, and everybody said:

"What a beautiful child! He looks like his grandfather Moses!"

That pleased me, of course; and I would go and look at him, bending over him for a long while, and finding a still stronger resemblance to my father.

At three o'clock, the meats having been removed and the delicacies spread upon the table, as we came to the dessert, I went down to find a bottle of better wine, an old bottle of Rousillon which I dug out from under the others, all covered with dust and cobwebs. I took it up carefully and placed it among the flowers on the table, saying:

"You thought the other wine very good; what will you say to this?"

Then Burguet smiled, for old wine was his special delight; he stretched up his hand and exclaimed:

"Oh! noble wine, the consoler, the restorer and benefactor of poor men in this vale of misery! Oh, venerable bottle, thou bearest all the signs of old nobility!"

He said this with his mouth full, and everybody laughed.

I asked Sorlé to bring the corkscrew.

As she was rising, suddenly trumpets sounded without, and we all listened and asked, "What is that?"

At the same time the sound of many horses' steps came up the street, and the earth and the houses trembled under an enormous weight.

Everybody sprang up, throwing down their napkins and rushing to the windows.

And from the French gate to the little square we saw trains of artillerymen advancing, with their great shakos covered with oil-cloth, and their saddles in sheepskins and driving caissons full of round shot, shells and intrenching tools.

Imagine, Fritz, my thoughts at that moment?

"This is war, my friends!" said Burguet. "This is war! It is coming! Our turn has come, at the end of twenty years!"

I stood leaning down with my hand on the stone, and thought:

"Now the enemy cannot delay coming. These are sent to fortify the place. And what if the Allies surround us before I have received my spirits of wine? What if the Austrians or Russians should stop the wagons and seize them? I should have to pay for it all the same, and I should not have a farthing left!"

I turned pale at the thought. Sorlé looked at me, undoubtedly having the same fears, but she said nothing.

We stood there till they all passed by. The street was full. Some old soldiers, Desmarets the Egyptian, Paradis the gunner, Rolfo, Faisard the sapper, of the Beresina, as he was called, and some others, cried "Vive l'Empereur!"

Children ran behind the wagons, repeating the cry, "Vive l'Empereur!" But the greater number, with closed lips and serious faces, looked on in silence.

When the last carriage had turned the Fouquet corner, all the crowd returned with bowed heads; and we in the room looked at each other, with no wish to continue the feast.

"You are not well, Moses," said Burguet. "What is the matter?"

"I am thinking of all the evils which are coming to the city."

"Bah! don't be afraid," he replied. "We shall be strongly defended! And then, God help us! what can't be cured must be endured! Come! cheer up; this old wine will keep up our spirits."

We resumed our places. I opened the bottle, and it was as Burguet said. The old Rousillon did us good, and we began to laugh.

Burguet called out:

"To the health of the little Esdras! May the Lord cover him with his right hand!"

And the glasses clinked. Some one exclaimed: "May he long rejoice the hearts of his grandfather Moses and his grandmother Sorlé! To their health!"

We ended by looking at everything in rose-color, and glorifying the Emperor, who was has tening to defend us, and was soon going to crush all the beggars beyond the Rhine.

But it is equally true that, when we separated about five o'clock, everybody had become serious, and Burguet himself, when he shook hands with me at the foot of the stairs, looked anxious.

"We shall have to send home our pupils," said he, "and we must sit with our arms folded."

The Saverne people, with Zeffen, Baruch, and the children, got into their carriage, and started silently for home.

IV.

FATHER MOSES COMPELLED TO BEAR ARMS.

All this, Fritz, was but the beginning of troubles.

You should have seen the city the next morning, at about eleven o'clock, when the engineering officers had finished inspecting the ramparts, and the tidings suddenly spread that there were needed seventy-two platforms inside the bastions, three bomb-proof block-houses, for thirty men each, at the right and left of the German gate, ten palankas with battlements forming stronghold intrenchments for forty men, and four blindages upon the great square of the mayoralty to shelter each a hundred and ten men; and when it was known that the citizens would be obliged to work at all these, to provide themselves with shovels, pickaxes, and wheelbarrows, and the peasants to bring trees with their own horses!

As for Sorlé, Sâfel, and myself, we did not even know what blindages and palankas were; we asked our neighbor Bailly, an old armorer, what they were for, and he answered with a smile:

"You will find out, neighbor, when you hear the balls roar and the shells hiss. It would take too long to explain. You will see, by and by; never too late to learn."

Imagine how the people looked! I remember that everybody ran to the square, where our mayor, Baron Parmentier, made a speech. We ran there with all the rest.

Sorlé held me by the arm, and Sâfel by the skirt of my coat.

There, in front of the mayoralty, the whole city, men, women, and children, formed in a semicircle, and listened in the deepest silence, now and then crying all together, "Vive l'Empereur!"

Parmentier, a tall, thin man, in a sky-blue dress-coat, a white cravat, and the tri-colored sash around his waist, stood on the top of the steps of the guard-house, with the members of the municipal council behind him, under the arch, and shouted out:

"Phalsburgians! The time has come in which to show your devotion to the Empire. A year ago all Europe was with us, now all Europe is against us. We should have everything to fear without the energy and power of the people. He who will not do his duty now will be a traitor to his country! Inhabitants of Phalsburg, show what you are! Remember that your children have perished through the treachery of the allies. Avenge them! Let every one be obedient to the military authority, for the sake of the safety of France," etc.

Only to hear him made one's flesh creep, and I said to myself:

"Now there will not be time for the spirits of wine to get here—that is plain! The allies are on their way!"

Elias the butcher, and Kalmes Levi the ribbon-merchant, were standing near us. Instead of crying "Vive l'Empereur!" with the rest, they said to each other;

"Good! we are not barons, you and I! Barons, counts, and dukes have but to defend themselves. Are we to think only of their interests?"

But all the old soldiers, and especially those of the Republic, old Goulden, the clockmaker, Desmarels, the Egyptian—creatures with not a hair left on their heads, nor as much as four teeth to hold their pipes—these creatures fell in with the mayor, and cried out:

"Vive la France! We must defend ourselves to the death!"

I saw several looking askance at Kalmes Levy, and I whispered to him:

"Keep still, Kalmes! For heaven's sake, keep still! They will tear you in pieces!"

It was true. The old men gave him terrible looks; they grew pale, and their cheeks shook.

Then Kalmes stopped talking, and even left the crowd to return home. But Elias stayed till the end of the speech, and, as the whole mass of people were going down the main street, shouting "Vive l'Empereur!" he could not help saying to the old clockmaker:

"What! you, Mr. Goulden, a reasonable man, who have never wanted anything of the Emperor, you are now going to take his part, and cry out that we must defend ourselves till death! Is it our business to be soldiers? Have not we furnished enough soldiers to the Empire these last ten years? Have not enough men been killed? Must we give, besides, our own blood to support barons, counts, and dukes?"

But old Goulden did not let him finish, and

replied, as if indignant: "Listen, Elias! try to keep still! The thing now to be done is not to know what is right or wrong — it is to save France. I warn you, that if you try to discourage others, it will be bad for you. Believe me — go!"

Already a number of superannuated soldiers were gathered round us, and Elias had only time to retreat by the opposite lane.

From this time public notices, requisitions, forced labors, domiciliary visits for tools and wheelbarrows, came one after another, incessantly. A man was nothing in his own house; the officers of the place assumed authority over everything: only to be sure, they gave receipts.

All the tools from my storehouse of iron were in use on the ramparts. Fortunately I had sold a good many beforehand, for these tickets in place of my wares would have ruined me.

From time to time the mayor made a speech, and the governor, a fat man, covered with pimples, expressed his satisfaction to the citizens; that made up for their money!

When my time came to take the pickaxe and draw the wheelbarrow, I arranged with Carabin, the wood-sawyer, to take my place for thirty sous

Ah, what misery! Such a time will never come again.

While the governor commanded us within the city, the soldiers were always outside to superintend the peasants. The road to Lutzelburg was but one line of carts, laden with old oaks for building blockhouses. These are large sentry-boxes, or turrets, built up of solid trunks of trees, laid crosswise one upon another, and then covered with earth. These are more solid than an arch. Shells and bombs might rain upon them without disturbing anything within, as I found afterward.

These trees were also used to make lines of enormous palisades, pointed and pierced with holes for firing; these are what they call palankas.

I seem still to hear the shouts of the peasants, the neighing of the horses, the strokes of the whips, and all the other noises, which never stopped, day or night.

My only consolation was in thinking, "If the spirits of wine comes now, it will be well defended; the Austrians, Prussians, and Russians will not drink it here!"

Every morning Sorlé expected to receive the invoice.

One Sabbath day we had the curiosity to go and

see the works of the bastions. Everybody was talking about it, and Sâfel kept coming to me, saying: "The work is going on; they are filling the shells in front of the arsenal; they are taking out the cannon; they are mounting them on the ramparts!"

We could not keep the child away. He had nothing to sell now under the market, and it would be too tedious for him to stay at home. He scoured the city, and brought us back the news.

On this day, then, having heard that forty-two pieces were ranged in battery, and that they were continuing the work upon the bastion of the infantry-barracks, I told Sorlé to bring her shawl, and we would go and see.

We first went down to the French gate. Hundreds of wheelbarrows were going up the ramparts of the bastion, from which could be seen the road to Metz on the right and the road to Paris on the left.

There, above, crowds of laborers, soldiers and citizens, were heaping up a mass of earth in the form of a triangle, at least twenty-five feet in height, and two hundred in length and breadth.

An engineering officer had discovered with his spy-glass that this bastion was commanded by the hill opposite, and so everybody was set to work to place two pieces on a level with the hill.

It was the same everywhere else. The interior of these bastions, with their platforms, were shut in all around, for seven feet from the ground, like rooms. Nothing could fall into them except from the sky. In the turf, however, were dug narrow openings, larger without, like funnels; the mouths of the cannon, which were raised upon immense carriages, were drawn out through these apertures; they could be pushed forward and backward, and turned in all directions, by means of great levers passed in rings over the hind wheels of the carriages.

I had not yet heard the sound of these forty-eight pounders. But the mere sight of them on their platforms gave me a terrible idea of their power. Even Sorlé said: "It is fine, Moses; it is well done!"

She was right, for within the bastions all was in complete order; not a weed remained, and upon the sides were piled great bags filled with earth to protect the artillerymen.

But what lost labor! and to think that every firing of these large guns costs at least a louis— money spent to kill our fellow-men!

In fine the people worked at these things with more enthusiasm than if they were gathering in their own harvests. I have often thought that if the French bestowed as much pains, good sense, and courage upon matters of peace, they would be the richest and happiest people in the world. Yes, they would long ago have surpassed the English and Americans. But when they have toiled and economized, when they have opened roads everywhere, built magnificent bridges, dug out harbors and canals, and riches come to them from all quarters, suddenly the fury of war possesses them, and in three or four years they ruin themselves with grand armies, with cannon, with powder, with bullets, with men, and become poorer than before. A few soldiers are their masters, and look down upon them. This is all it profits them!

In the midst of all this, news from Mayence, from Strasburg, from Paris, came by the dozens; we could not go into the street without seeing a courier pass. They all stopped before the Bockhold house, near the German gate, where the governor lived. A circle formed around the house, the courier mounted, then the news spread through the city that the allies were concentrated at Frankfort, that our troops guarded the islands of the

Rhine; that the conscripts from 1803 to 1814 were recalled; that those of 1815 would form the reserve corps at Metz, at Bordeaux, at Turin; that the deputies were going to assemble; then, that the gates had been shut upon them, etc., etc.

There came also smugglers of all sorts from Graufthal, Pirmasens, and Kaiserslautern, with Franz Sépel, the one-armed man, at their head, and others from the villages around, who secretly scattered the proclamations of Alexander, Francis Joseph and Frederic William, saying "that they did not make war upon France, but upon the Emperor alone, to prevent his further desolation of Europe." They spoke of the abolition of duties, and of taxes of all sorts. The people at night did not know what to think.

But one fine morning it was all explained. It was the eighth or ninth of December. I had just risen, and was putting on my clothes, when I heard the rolling of a drum at the corner of the main street.

It was cold, but nevertheless I opened the window and leaned out to hear the announcements. Parmentier opened his paper, young Engelheider kept up his drum-beating, and the people assembled.

Then Parmentier read that the governor of

the place ordered all citizens to present themselves at the mayoralty between eight in the morning and six in the evening, without fail, to receive their muskets and cartridge-boxes, and that those who did not come, would be court-martialed.

There was the end at last! Every one who was able to march was on his way, and the old men were to defend the fortifications; sober-minded men—citizens—men accustomed to living quietly at home, and attending to their own affairs! now they must mount the ramparts and every day run the risk of losing their lives!

Sorlé looked at me without a word, and indignation made me also speechless. Not till after a quarter of an hour, when I was dressed, did I say:

"Make the soup ready. I am going to the mayoralty to get my musket and cartridge-box."

Then she exclaimed: "Moses, who would have believed that you would have to go and fight at your age? Oh! what misery!"

And I answered: "It is the Lord's will."

Then I started with a sad heart. Little Sâfel followed me.

As I arrived at the corner of the market, Burguet was coming down the mayoralty steps, which swarmed with men; he had his musket on his shoulder, and said with a smile:

"Ah, well, Moses! We are going to turn Maccabees in our old age?"

His cheerfulness encouraged me, and I replied:

"Burguet, how is it they can take rational men, heads of families, and make them destroy themselves? I cannot comprehend it; no, there is no sense in it!"

"Ah," said he, "what would you have? If they can't get thrushes, they must take blackbirds."

I could not smile at his pleasantries, and he said:

"Come, Moses, don't be so disconsolate; this is only a formality. We have troops enough for active service; we shall have only to mount guard. If sorties are to be made, or attacks repulsed, they will not take you; you are not of an age to run, or to give a bayonet stroke! You are gray and bald. Don't be troubled!"

"Yes," I said, "that is very true, Burguet, I am broken down—more so, perhaps, than you think.

"That is well," said he, "but go and take your musket and cartridge-box."

"And are we not going to stay in the barracks?"

"No, no!" he cried, laughing aloud, "we are going to live quietly at home."

He shook hands with me, and I went under the arch of the mayoralty. The stairway was crowded with people, and we heard names called out.

And there, Fritz, you should have seen the looks of the Robinots, the Gourdiers, the Mariners, that mass of tilers, knife-grinders, house-painters, people who, every day, in ordinary times, would take off their caps to you to get a little work— you should have seen them straighten themselves up, look at you pityingly over the shoulder, blow in their cheeks, and call out:

"Ah, Moses, is it thou? Thou wilt make a comical soldier. He! he! he! They will cut thy mustaches according to regulation!"

And such-like nonsense.

Yes, everything was changed; these former bullies had been named in advance sergeants, sergeant-majors, corporals, and the rest of us were nothing at all. War upsets everything; the first become last, and the last first. It is not good sense but discipline which carries the day. The man who scrubbed your floor yesterday, because he was too stupid to gain a living any other way, becomes your sergeant, and if he tells you that white is black, you must let it be so.

At last, after waiting an hour, some one called out, "Moses!" and I went up.

The great hall above was full of people. They all exclaimed:

"Moses! Wilt thou come, Moses? Ah, see him! He is the old guard! Look now, how he is built! Thou shalt be ensign, Moses! Thou shalt lead us on to victory!"

And the fools laughed, nudging each others' elbows. I passed on, without answering or even looking at them.

In the room at the farther end, where the names were drawn at conscriptions, Governor Moulin, Commandant Petitgenet, the mayor, Frichard, secretary of the mayoralty, Rollin, captain of apparel, and six or seven other superannuated men, crippled with rheumatism, brought from all parts of the world, were met in council, some sitting, the rest standing.

These old ones began to laugh as they saw me come in. I heard them say to one another: "He is strong yet! Yes, he is all right."

So they talked, one after another. I thought to myself: "Say what you like, you will not make me think that you are twenty years old, or that you are handsome."

But I kept silence.

Suddenly the governor, who was talking with the mayor in a corner, turned around, with his great chapeau awry, and looking at me, said:

"What do you intend to do with such a patriarch? You see very well that he can hardly stand."

I was pleased, in spite of it all, and began to cough.

"Good, good!" said he, "you may go home take care of your cold!"

I had taken four steps toward the door, when Frichard, the secretary of the mayoralty, called out:

"It is Moses! The Jew Moses, Colonel, who has sent his two boys off to America! The oldest should be in the service."

This wretch of a Frichard had a grudge against me, because we had the same business of selling old clothes under the market, and the country people almost always preferred buying of me; he had a mortal grudge against me, and that is why he began to inform against me.

The governor exclaimed at once: "Stop a min

ute! Ah ha, old fox! You send your boys to America to escape conscription! Very well! Give him his musket, cartridge-box, and sabre."

Indignation against Frichard choked me. I would have spoken, but the wretch laughed and kept on writing at the desk; so I followed the gendarme Werner to a side room, which was filled with muskets, sabres, and cartridge-boxes.

Werner himself hung a cartridge-box crosswise on my back, and gave me a musket, saying:

"Go, Moses, and try always to answer to the call."

I went down through the crowd so indignant that I heard no longer the shouts of laughter from the rabble.

On reaching home I told Sorlé what had happened. She was very pale as she listened. After a moment, she said: "This Frichard is the enemy of our race; he is an enemy of Israel. I know it; he detests us! But just now, Moses, do not say a word; do not let him see that you are angry; it would please him too much. By and by you can have your revenge! You will have a chance. And if not yourself, your children, your grandchildren; they shall all know what this wretch has done to their grandfather—they shall know it!"

She clenched her hand, and little Säfel listened

This was all the comfort she could give me. I thought as she did, but I was so angry that I would have given half my fortune to ruin the wretch. All that day, and in the night, too, I exclaimed more than twenty times:

"Ah, the scoundrel!—I was going—they had said to me, 'You may go!'—He is the cause of all my misery!"

You cannot imagine, Fritz, how I have always hated that man. Never have my wife and I forgotten the harm he did us—never shall my children forget it.

V.

FATHER MOSES RECEIVES WELCOME NEWS.

The next day we must answer to the call before the mayoralty. All the children in town surrounded us and whistled. Fortunately, the blindages of the Place d'Armes were not finished, so that we went to learn our exercises in the large court of the college, near the *chemin de ronde* at the corner of the powder-house. As the pupils had been dismissed for some time, the place was at liberty.

Imagine to yourself this large court filled with citizens in bonnets, coats, cloaks, vests, and breeches, obliged to obey the orders of their former tinkers, chimney-sweeps, stable-boys, now turned into corporals, sergeants, and sergeant-majors. Imagine these peaceable men, in fours, in sixes, in tens, stretching out their legs in concert, and marching to the step, "One—*two!* One—*two!* Halt! Steady!" while others, marching backward, frowning, called out insolently: "Moses, dress thy shoulders!" "Moses, bring thy nose into line!" "Attention, Moses! Carry arms! Ah, old shoe, thou'lt never be good for anything! Can any one be so stupid at his age? Look—just look! Thunder! Canst thou not do that? One—*two!* What an old blockhead! Come, begin again! Carry arms!"

This is the way my own cobbler, Monborne, ordered me about. I believe he would have beaten me if it had not been for Captain Vigneron.

All the rest treated their old patrons in the same way. You would have said that it had always been so—that they had always been sergeants and we had always been soldiers. I heaped up gall enough against this rabble to last fifty years.

They in fine were the masters! And the only time that I remember ever to have struck my own son, Sâfel, this Monborne was the cause of it. All the children climbed upon the wall of the *chemin de ronde* to look at us and laugh at us. On looking up, I saw Sâfel among them, and made a sign of displeasure with my finger. He went down at once; but at the close of the exercise, when we were ordered to break ranks before the town-house, I was seized with anger as I saw him coming toward me, and I gave him two good boxes on the ear, and said: "Go—hiss and mock at your father, like Shem, instead of bringing a garment to cover his nakedness—go!"

He wept bitterly, and in this state I went home. Sorlé seeing me come in looking very pale, and the little one following me at a distance, sobbing, came down at once to the door, and asked what was the matter. I told her how angry I was, and went up stairs.

Sorlé reproved Sâfel still more severely, and he came and begged my pardon. I granted it with all my heart, as you may suppose. But when I thought that the exercises were to be repeated every day, I would gladly have abandoned everything if I could possibly have taken with me my house and wares.

Yes, the worst thing I know of is to be ordered about by bullies who cannot restrain themselves when chance sets them up for a moment, and who are not capable of receiving the idea that in this life everybody has his turn.

I should say too much if I continued on this head. I would rather go on.

The Lord granted me a great consolation. I had scarcely laid aside my cartridge-box and musket, so as to sit at the table, when Sorlé smilingly handed me a letter.

"Read that, Moses," said she, "and you will feel better."

I opened and read it. It was the notice from Pézenas that my dozen pipes of spirits were on their way. I drew a long breath.

"Ah! that is good, now!" I exclaimed; "the spirits are coming by the ordinary conveyance; they will be here in three weeks. We hear nothing from the direction of Strasburg and Sarrebruck; the allies are collecting still, but they do not move; my spirits of wine are safe! They will sell well! It is a grand thing!"

I smiled, and was quite myself again, when Sorlé pushed the arm-chair toward me, saying; "And what do you think of *that*, Moses?"

She gave me, as she spoke, a second letter, covered with large stamps, and at the first glance I recognized the handwriting of my two sons, Frômel and Itzig.

It was a letter from America! My heart swelled with joy, and I silently thanked the Lord, deeply moved by this great blessing. I said: "The Lord is good. His understanding is infinite. He delighteth not in the strength of a horse; he taketh not pleasure in the legs of a man. He taketh pleasure in those that hope in his mercy."

Thus I spoke to myself while I read the letter, in which my sons praised America, the true land of commerce, the land of enterprising men, where everything is free, where there are no taxes or impositions, because people are not brought up for war, but for peace; the land, Fritz, where every man becomes, through his own labor, his intelligence, his economy, and his good intentions, what he deserves to be, and every one takes his proper place, because no important matter is decided without the consent of all;—a just and sensible thing, for where all contribute, all should give their opinions.

This was one of their first letters. Frômel and Itzig wrote me that they had made so much money in a year, that they need no longer carry their own packs, but had three fine mules, and that they had just opened at Catskill, near Albany, in the State of New York, an establishment for the exchange of European fabrics with cowhides, which were very abundant in that region.

Their business was prospering, and they were respected in the town and its vicinity. While Frômel was travelling on the road with their three mules, Itzig staid at home, and when Itzig went in his turn his brother had charge of the shop.

They already knew of our misfortunes, and thanked the Lord for having given them such parents, to save them from destruction. They would have liked to have us with them, and after what had just happened, in being maltreated by a Monborne, you can believe that I should have been very glad to be there. But it was enough to receive such good news, and in spite of all our misfortunes, I said to myself, as I thought of Frichard: "But it is only to me that you can be an ass! You may harm me here, but you can't hurt my boys. You are nothing but a miserable secretary of mayoralty, while I am going to sell my spirits of wine. I shall gain double and treble. I will put my little Sâfel at your side, under the market, and he will beckon to everybody that is going into your shop; and he will sell to them at cost-price rather than lose their custom, and he will make you die of anger."

The tears came into my eyes as I thought of it, and I ended by embracing Sorlé, who smiled, full of satisfaction.

We pardoned Sâfel over again, and he promised to go no more with the cursed race. Then, after dinner, I went down to my cellar, one of the finest in the city, twelve feet high and thirty-five feet long, all built of hewn stone, under the main street. It was as dry as an oven, and even improved wine in the long run.

As my spirits of wine might arrive before the end of the month, I arranged four large beams to hold the pipes, and saw that the well, cut in the rock, had enough water for mixing it.

On going up about four o'clock, I perceived the old architect, Krômer, who was walking across the market, his measuring-stick under his arm.

"Ah!" said I, "come down a minute into my cellar; do you think it will be safe against the bombs?"

We went down together. He examined it, measured the stones and the thickness of the arch with his stick, and said: "You have six feet of earth over the key-stone. When the bombs enter here, Moses, it will be all over with all of us. You may sleep with both ears shut."

We took a good drink of wine from the spout, and went up in good spirits.

Just as we set foot on the pavement, a door in the main street opened with a crash, and there was a sound of glass broken. Krômer raised his nose, and said: "Look yonder, Moses, at Camus' steps! Something is going on."

We stopped and saw at the top of the railed staircase a sergeant of veterans, in a gray coat, with his musket dangling, dragging Father Camus by the collar. The poor old man clung to the door with both hands to keep himself from falling; he succeeded at last in getting loose, by tearing the collar from his coat, and the door shut with a noise like thunder.

"If war begins now between citizens and soldiers," said Krömer, "the Germans and Russians will have fine sport."

The sergeant, seeing the door shut and bolted within, tried to force it open with blows from the butt-end of his musket, which caused a great uproar; the neighbors came out, and the dogs barked. We were watching it all, when we saw Burguet come along the passage in front, and begin to talk vehemently with the sergeant. At first the man did not seem to hear him, but after a moment he raised his musket to his shoulder with a rough movement, and went down to the street, with his shoulders up and his face dark and furious. He passed by us like a wild boar. He was a veteran with three chevrons, sunburnt, with a gray mus tache, large straight wrinkles the whole length of his cheeks, and a square chin. He muttered as he passed us, and went into the little inn of the Three Pigeons.

Burguet followed at a distance, with his broad hat down to his eyebrows, wrapped in his beaver-cloth great coat, his head thrown back, and his hands in his pockets. He smiled.

"Well," said I, "what has been going on at Camus'?"

"Oh!" said he, "it is Sergeant Trubert, of the fifth company of veterans, who had just been playing his tricks. The old fellow wants everything to go by rule and measure. In the last fortnight he has had five different lodgings, and cannot get along with anybody. Everybody complains of him, but he always makes excuses which the Governor and Commandant think excellent."

"And at Camus' house?"

"Camus has not too much room for his own family. He wished to send the sergeant to the inn; but the sergeant had already chosen Camus' bed to sleep in, had spread his cloak upon it, and said, 'My billet is for this place. I am very comfortable here, and do not wish to change.' Old Camus was vexed, and finally, as you have just seen, the sergeant tried to pull him out, and beat him."

Burguet smiled, but Krömer said: "Yes, all that is laughable. And yet when we think of what such people must have done on the other side of the Rhine!"

"Ah!" exclaimed Burguet, "it was not very pleasant for the Germans, I am sure. But it is time to go and read the newspaper. God grant that the time for paying our old debts may not have come! Good-evening, gentlemen."

He continued his walk on the side of the square. Krömer went toward his own house, while I shut the two doors of my cellar; after which I went home.

This was the tenth of December. It was already very cold. Every night, after five or six o'clock, the roofs and pavements were covered with frost. There was no more noise without, because people kept at home, around their stoves.

I found Sorlé in the kitchen, preparing our supper. The red flame flickered upon the hearth around the sauce-pan. These things are now before my eyes, Fritz — the mother, washing the plates at the stone sink, near the gray window; little Sâfel blowing in his big iron pipe, his cheeks round as an apple, his long curly hair all disordered, and myself sitting on the stool, holding a coal to light my pipe. Yes, it all seems here present!

We said nothing. We were happy in thinking of the spirits of wine that were coming, of the boys who were doing so well, of the good supper that was cooking. And who would ever have thought, then, that twenty-five days afterwards the city would be surrounded by enemies, and shells hissing in the air?

VI.

A DISAGREEABLE GUEST.

Now, Fritz, I am going to tell you something which has often made me think that the Lord takes an interest in our affairs, and that he orders everything for the best. At first it seems dreadful, and we exclaim, "Lord have mercy on us!" and afterward we are surprised to find that it has all been for our good.

You know that Frichard, the secretary of the mayoralty, disliked me. He was a little, yellow, dried up old man, with a red wig, flat ears, and hollow cheeks. This rascal was bent on doing me an injury, and he soon found an opportunity.

As the time of the blockade drew nearer, people were more and more anxious to sell, and the day after I received the good news from America—it was Friday, a market-day—so many of the Alsacian and Lorraine people came with their great dossers and panniers of fruit, eggs, butter, cheese, poultry, etc., that the market-place was crowded with them.

Everybody wanted money, to hide it in his cellar, or under a tree in the neighboring wood. You know that large sums were lost at that time; treasures which are now discovered from year to year, at the foot of oaks and beeches, hidden because it was feared that the Germans and Russians would pillage and destroy everything, as we had done to them. The men died, or perhaps could not find the place where they had hidden their money, and so it remained buried in the ground.

This day, the eleventh of December, it was very cold ; the frost penetrated to the very marrow of your bones, but it had not yet begun to snow. Very early in the morning, I went down, shivering, with my woollen waistcoat buttoned up to my throat, and my seal-skin cap drawn down over my ears.

Both the little and the great squares were already swarming with people, shouting and disputing about prices. I had only time to open my shop, and to hang up my large scales in the arch, before a crowd of country people stood about the door, some asking for nails, others iron for forging ; and some bringing their own old iron with the hope of selling it.

They knew that if the enemy came there would be no way of entering the city, and that was what brought the crowd, some to sell and others to buy.

I opened shop and began to weigh. We heard

the patrols passing without; the guard was everywhere doubled, the drawbridges in good condition, and the outside barriers fortified anew. We were not yet declared to be in a state of siege, but we were like the bird on the branch; the last news from Mayence, Sarrebruck, and Strasburg announced the arrival of the allies on the other bank of the Rhine.

As for me, I thought of nothing but my spirits of wine, and all the time I was selling, weighing, and handling money, it was never out of my mind. It had, as it were, taken root in my brain.

This had lasted about an hour, when suddenly Burguet appeared at my door, under the little arch, behind the crowd of country people, and said to me:

"Moses, come here a minute, I have something to say to you."

I went out.

"Let us go into your passage," said he.

I was much surprised, for he looked very grave. The peasants behind called out:

"We have no time to lose. Make haste, Moses!"

But I paid no attention. In the passage Burguet said to me:

"I have just come from the mayoralty, where they are busy in making out a report to the prefect in regard to the state of feeling among our popula tion, and I accidentally heard that they are going to send Sergeant Trubert to your house."

This was indeed a blow for me. I exclaimed:

"I don't want him! I don't want him! I have lodged six men in the last fortnight, and it isn't my turn."

He answered:

"Be quiet, and don't talk so loud. You will only make the matter worse."

I repeated:

"Never, never shall this sergeant enter my house! It is abominable! A quiet man like myself, who has never harmed any one, and who asks nothing but peace!"

While I was speaking, Sorlé, on her way to market, with her basket on her arm, came down, and asked what was the matter.

"Listen, Madame Sorlé," said Burguet to her: "be more reasonable than your husband! I can understand his indignation, and yet for all that, when a thing is inevitable we must submit to it. Frichard dislikes you; he is secretary of the mayoralty; he distributes the billets for quartering soldiers according to a list. Very well; he sends you Sergeant Trubert, a violent, bad man, I allow, but he needs lodging as well as the others. To everything which I have said in your favor, Frichard has always replied: 'Moses is rich. He has sent away his boys to escape conscription. He ought to pay for them.' The mayor, the governor, everybody thinks he is right. So, you see, I tell you as a friend, the more resistance you make, so much the more the sergeant will affront you, and Frichard laugh at you, and there will be no help for it. Be reasonable!"

I was still more angry on finding that I owed these misfortunes to Frichard. I would have exclaimed, but my wife laid her hand on my arm, and said:

"Let me speak, Moses. Monsieur Burguet is right, and I am much obliged to him for telling us beforehand. Frichard has a spite against us. Very well; he must pay for it all, and we will settle with him by-and-bye. Now, when is the sergeant coming?"

"At noon," replied Burguet.

"Very well," said my wife; "he has a right to lodging, fire, and candles. We can't dispute that; but Frichard shall pay for it all."

She was pale, and I listened, for I saw that she was right.

"Be quiet, Moses," she said to me afterward, "and don't say a word; let me manage it."

"This is what I had to say to you," said Burguet, "it is an abominable trick of Frichard's. I will see, by-and-bye, if it is possible to rid you of the sergeant. Now I must go back to my post."

Sorlé had just started for the market. Burguet pressed my hand, and as the peasants grew more impatient in their cries, I had to go back to my scales.

I was full of rage. I sold that day more than two hundred francs' worth of iron, but my indignation against Frichard, and my fear of the sergeant, took away all pleasure in anything. I might have sold ten times more without feeling any better.

"Ah! the rascal!" I said to myself; "he gives me no rest. I shall have no peace in this city."

As the clock struck twelve the market closed, and people went away by the French gate. I shut up my shop and went home, thinking to myself:

"Now I shall be nothing in my own house; this Trubert is going to rule everything. He will look down upon us as if we were Germans or Spaniards."

I was in despair. But in the midst of my despair on the staircase, I suddenly perceived an odor of good things from the kitchen, and I went up in surprise, for I smelt fish and roast, as if it were a feast day.

I was going into the kitchen, when Sorlé appeared and said:

"Go into your chamber, shave yourself, and put on a clean shirt."

I saw, at the same time, that she was dressed in her Sabbath clothes, with her ear-rings, her green skirt, and her red silk neckerchief.

"But why must I shave, Sorlé?" I exclaimed.

"Go quick; you have no time to lose!" replied she.

This woman had so much good sense, she had so many times set things right by her ready wit, that I said nothing more, and went into my bedroom to shave myself and put on a clean shirt.

As I was putting on my shirt I heard little Sâfel cry out:

"Here he is, mama! here he is!"

Then steps were heard on the stairs, and a rough voice called:

"Holla! you folks. Ho!"

I thought to myself: "It is the sergeant," and I listened.

"Ah! here is our sergeant!" cried Sâfel, triumphantly.

"Oh! that is good," replied my wife, in a cheerful tone. "Come in, Mr. Sergeant, come in! We were expecting you. I knew that we were to have the honor of having a sergeant; we were glad to hear it, because we have had only common soldiers before. Be so good as to come in, Mr. Sergeant."

She spoke in this way as if she were really pleased, and I thought to myself:

"O Sorlé, Sorlé! You shrewd woman! You sensible woman! I see through it now. I see your cunning. You are going to mollify this rascal! Ah, Moses! what a wife you have! Congratulate yourself! Congratulate yourself!"

I hastened to dress myself, laughing all the while; and I heard this brute of a sergeant say:

"Yes, yes! It is all very well. But that isn't the point! Show me my room, my bed. You can't pay me with fine speeches; people know Sergeant Trubert too well for that."

"Certainly, Mr. Sergeant, certainly," replied my wife, "here is your room and your bed. See, it is the best we have."

Then they went into the passage, and I heard Sorlé open the door of the handsome room which Baruch and Zeffen occupied when they came to Phalsburg.

I followed them softly. The sergeant thrust his fist into the bed to feel if it was soft. Sorlé and Sâfel looked on smilingly behind him. He examined every corner with a scowl. You never saw such a face, Fritz; a gray bristling moustache, a long thin nose, hooked over the mouth; a yellow skin, full of wrinkles: he dragged the butt-end of his gun on the floor, without seeming to notice anything, and muttered ill-naturedly:

"Hem! hem! What is that down there?"

"It is the wash-basin, Mr. Sergeant."

"And these chairs, are they strong? Will they bear anything?"

He knocked them rudely down. It was evident he wanted to find fault with something.

On turning round he saw me, and looking at me sideways, asked:

"Are you the citizen?"

"Yes, sergeant; I am."

"Ah!"

He put his gun in a corner, threw his knapsack on the table, and said:

"That will do! You may go."

Sâfel had opened the kitchen door, and the good smell of the roast came into the room.

"Mr. Sergeant," said Sorlé very pleasantly, "allow me to ask a favor of you."

"You!" said he looking at her over his shoulder, "ask a favor of me!"

"Yes. It is that since you now lodge with us, and will be in some respects one of the family, you will give us the pleasure of dining with us, at least for once."

"Ah, ah!" said he, turning his nose toward the kitchen, "that is another thing!"

He seemed to be considering whether to grant us this favor or not. We waited for him to answer, when he gave another sniff and threw his cartridge-box on the bed, saying:

"Well, so be it! We will go and see!"

"Wretch!" thought I, "if I could make you eat potatoes!"

But Sorlé seemed satisfied, and said:

"This way, Mr. Sergeant; this way, if you please."

When we went into the dining-room I saw that everything was prepared as if for a prince; the floor swept, the table carefully laid, a white table-cloth, and our silver knives and forks.

Sorlé placed the sergeant in my arm-chair at the head of the table, which seemed to him the most natural thing in the world.

Our servant brought in the large tureen and took off the cover; the odor of a good cream soup filled the room, and we began our dinner.

Fritz, I could tell you everything we had for dinner; but believe me, neither you nor I ever had a better. We had a roasted goose, a magnificent pike, sour-kraut, everything, in fact, which could be desired for a grand dinner, and all served by Sorlé in the most perfect manner. We had, too, four bottles of Beaujolais warmed in napkins, as was the custom in winter, and an abundant dessert.

Well! do you believe that the rascal once had the grace to seem pleased with all this? Do you believe that all through this dinner, which lasted nearly two hours, he once thought of saying, "This pike is excellent!" or, "This fat goose is well cooked!" or, "You have very good wine!" or any of the other things which we know are pleasant for a host to hear, and which repay a good cook for his trouble? No, Fritz, not once! You would have supposed that he had such dinners every day. The more even that my wife flattered him, and the more kindly she spoke to him, the more he rebuffed her, the more he scowled, the more defiantly he looked at us, as if we wanted to poison him.

From time to time I looked indignantly at Sorlé, but she kept on smiling; she kept on giving the nicest bits to the sergeant; she kept on filling his glass.

Two or three times I wanted to say, "Ah, Sorlé, what a good cook you are! How nice this forcemeat is!" But suddenly the sergeant would look down upon me as if to say, "What does that signify? Perhaps you want to give me lessons? Don't I know better than you do whether a thing is good or bad?"

So I kept silence. I could have wished him—well, in worse company; I grew more and more indignant at every morsel which he swallowed in silence. Nevertheless Sorlé's example encouraged me to put a good face on the matter, and toward the end I thought, "Now, since the dinner is eaten, since it is almost over, we will go on, with God's help. Sorlé was mistaken, but it is all the same; her idea was a good one, except for such a rascal!"

And I myself ordered coffee; I went to the closet, too, to get some cherry-brandy and old rum.

"What is that?" asked the sergeant.

"Rum and cherry-brandy; old cherry-brandy from the 'Black Forest,'" I replied.

"Ah," said he winking, "everybody says, 'I have got some cherry-brandy from the Black Forest!' It is very easy to say; but they can't cheat Sergeant Trubert; we will see about this!"

In taking his coffee he twice filled his glass with cherry-brandy, and both times said, "He! he! We will see whether it is genuine."

I could have thrown the bottle at his head.

As Sorlé went to him to pour a third glassful, he rose and said, "That is enough; thank you! The posts are doubled. This evening I shall be on guard at the French gate. The dinner, to be sure, was not a bad one. If you give me such now and then, we can get along with each other."

He did not smile, and, indeed, seemed to be ridiculing us.

"We will do our best, Mr. Sergeant," replied Sorlé, while he went into his room and took his great coat to go out.

"We will see," said he as he went down-stairs, "We will see!"

Till now I had said nothing, but when he was down I exclaimed, "Sorlé, never, no never, was there such a rascal! We shall never get along with this man. He will drive us all from the house."

"Bah! bah! Moses," she replied, laughing, "I do not think as thou dost! I have quite the contrary idea; we will be good friends, thou'lt see, thou'lt see!"

"God grant it!" I said; "but I have not much hope of it."

She smiled as she took off the table-cloth, and gave me too a little confidence, for this woman had a good deal of shrewdness, and I acknowledged her sound judgment.

VII.

SERGEANT TRUBERT IN A NEW LIGHT.

You see, Fritz, what the common people had to endure in those days. Ah, well! just as we were performing extra service, while Monborne was commanding me at the drilling, while Sergeant Trubert was down upon me, while we were hearing of domiciliary visits of inspection to ascertain what provisions the citizens had—in the midst of all this, my dozen pipes of spirits of wine were being slowly wheeled over the road.

How I repented of having ordered them! How often I could have torn my hair as I thought that half my thirty years' gains were at the mercy of circumstances! How I prayed for the Emperor! How I ran every morning to the coffee-houses and ale-houses to learn the news, and how I trembled as I read!

Nobody knew what I suffered, not even Sorlé, for I kept it all from her. She was too keen-sighted not to perceive my anxiety, and sometimes she would say, "Come, Moses, have courage! All will come right—patience a little longer!"

But the rumors which came from Alsace, and German Lorraine, and Hundsruck, quite upset me: "They are coming! They will not dare to come! We are ready for them! They will take us by surprise! Peace is going to be made! They will pass by to-morrow! We shall have no fighting this winter! They can wait no longer! The Emperor is still in Paris! Marshal Victor is at Huninguen! They are impressing the custom-house officers, the forest-keepers, and the gendarmery! Some Spanish dragoons went down by Saverne yesterday! The mountaineers are to defend the Vosges! There will be fighting in Alsace!" etc., etc. Your head would have been turned, Fritz. In the morning the wind would blow one way and put you in good spirits; at night it would blow another way and you would be miserable.

And my spirits of wine were coming nearer and nearer, and at last arrived, in the midst of this conflict of news, which might any day turn into a conflict of bullets and shells. If it had not been for my other troubles I should have been beside myself. Fortunately, my indignation against Monborne and the other villains diverted my mind.

We heard nothing more of Sergeant Trubert

after the great dinner for the remainder of that day, and the night following, as he was on guard; but the next morning, as I was getting up, behold, he came up the stairs, with his musket on his shoulder; he opened the door and began to laugh, with his moustaches all white with frost. I had just put on my pantaloons, and looked at him in astonishment. My wife was still in her room.

"He! he! Father Moses," said he, in a good-natured voice, "It has been a dreadful cold night." He did not look or speak like the same person.

"Yes, sergeant," I replied, "it is December, and that is what we must expect."

"What we must expect," he repeated;—"all the more reason for taking a drop. Let us see, is there any more of that old cherry-brandy?"

He looked, as he spoke, as if he could see through me. I got up at once from my arm-chair, and ran to fetch the bottle: "Yes, yes, sergeant," I exclaimed, "there is more, drink and enjoy it."

As I said this, his face, still a little hard, seemed to smile all over. He placed his gun in a corner, and, standing up, handed me the glass, saying, "Pour out, Father Moses, pour out!"

I filled it brimfull. As I did so, he laughed quietly. His yellow face puckered up in hundreds of wrinkles at the corners of his eyes, and around his cheeks and moustaches and chin. He did not laugh so as to be heard, but his eyes showed his good humor.

"Famous cherry-brandy this, in truth, Father Moses!" he said as he drank it. "A body knows who has drank it in the Black Forest, where it cost nothing! Aren't you going to drink with me?"

"With pleasure," I answered. And we drank together. He looked at me all the time. Suddenly he said, with a mischievous look, "Hey, Father Moses, say, you were afraid of me yesterday?" He smiled as he spoke.

"Oh—Sergeant"—

"Come, come," said he, laying his hand upon my shoulder—"confess that I frightened you."

He smiled so pleasantly that I could not help saying: "Well, yes, a little!"

"He! he! he! I knew it very well," said he. "You had heard them say, 'Sergeant Trubert is a tough one!' You were afraid, and you gave me a dinner fit for a prince to coax me!"

He laughed aloud, and I ended by laughing too. Sorlé had heard all, in the next room, and now came to the door and said, "Good morning, Mr. Sergeant."

He exclaimed, "Father Moses, here is what may be called a woman! You can boast of having a spirited woman, a sly woman, slyer than you are, Father Moses; he, he, he! That is as it should be—that is as it should be!"

Sorlé was delighted.

"Oh! Mr. Sergeant," said she, "can you really think so?"

"Bah! bah!" he exclaimed. "You are a first-rate woman! I saw you when I first came, and said to myself, 'Take heed, Trubert! They make a fair pretense; it is a stratagem to send you to the hotel to sleep. We will let the enemy unmask his batteries!'

"Ha! ha! ha! You are nice folks. You gave me a dinner fit for a Marshal of the Empire. Now, Father Moses, I invite myself to take a small glass of cherry-brandy with you now and then. Put the bottle aside, by itself, it is excellent! And as for the rest, the room which you have given me is too handsome; I don't like such gewgaws; this fine furniture and these soft beds are good for women. What I want is a small room, like that at the side, two good chairs, a pine table, a plain bed with a mattress, paillasse, and coverings, and five or six nails in the wall for hanging my things. You just give me that!"

"Since you wish it, Mr. Sergeant."

"Yes, I wish it; the handsome room will be for state occasions."

"You will breakfast with us?" asked my wife, well pleased.

"I breakfast and dine at the cantine," replied the sergeant. "I do very well there; and I don't want to have good people go to any expense for me. When people respect an old soldier as he ought to be respected, when they treat him kindly, when they are like you,—Trubert, too, is what he ought to be."

"But, Mr. Sergeant!" said Sorlé.

"Call me Sergeant," said he, "I know you now. You are not like all the rabble of the city; rascals who have been growing rich while we have been off fighting; wretches who do nothing but heap up money and grow big at the expense of the army, who live on us, who are indebted to us for everything, and who send us to sleep in nests of vermin. Ah! a thousand million thunders!"

His face resumed its bad look; his moustaches shook with his anger, and I thought to myself, "What a good idea it was to treat him well! Sorlé's ideas are always good!"

But in a moment he relaxed, and laying his hand on my arm, he exclaimed:

"To think that you are Jews! a kind of abominable race; everything that is dirty and vile and niggardly! To think that you are Jews! It is true, is it not, that you are Jews?"

"Yes, sir," replied Sorlé.

"Well, upon my word, I am surprised to hear it," said he; "I have seen so many Jews, in Poland and Germany, that I thought to myself 'They are sending me to some Jews; they had better look out or I'll smash everything.'"

We kept silent in our mortification, and he added, "Come, we will say no more about that. You are good, honest people; I should be sorry to trouble you. Your hand, Father Moses!"

I gave him my hand.

"I like you," said he. "Now, Madame Moses, the side room!"

We showed him the small room that he asked for, and he went at once to fetch his knapsack from the other, saying as he went:

"Now I am among honest people! We shall have no difficulty in getting along together. You do not trouble me, I do not trouble you; I come in and go out, by day or night; it is Sergeant Trubert, that is enough. And now and then, in the morning, we will take our little glass; it is agreed, is it not, Father Moses?"

"Yes, sergeant."

"And here is the key of the house," said Sorlé.

"Very well; everything is arranged; now I am going to take a nap; good-bye, my friends."

"I hope you will sleep well, sergeant." We went out at once, and heard him lie down.

"You see, Moses, you see," whispered my wife, in the alley, "it has all come right."

"Yes," I replied, "all right, excellent; your plan was a good one; and now, if the spirits of wine only come, we shall be happy."

VIII.

FATHER MOSES' FIRST ENCOUNTER.

From that time the sergeant lived with us without troubling anybody. Every morning, before he went to his duties, he came and sat a few minutes in my room, and talked with me while he took his glass. He liked to laugh with Sâfel, and we called him "our sergeant," as if he were one of the family. He seemed to like to be with us; he was a careful man; he would not allow our *schabisboïë* to black his shoes; he cleaned his own buff-skins, and would not let any one touch his arms.

One morning, when I was going to answer to the call, he met me in the alley, and, seeing a little rust on my musket, he began to swear like the devil.

"Ah! Father Moses, if I had you in my company, it would go hard with you!"

"Yes," thought I; "but, thank God, I'm not."

Sorlé, leaning over the balustrades above, laughed heartily.

From that time the sergeant regularly inspected

my equipments; I must clean my gun over and over, take it to pieces, clean the barrel and furbish the bayonet, as if I expected to go and fight. And even when he knew how Monborne treated me, he also wanted to teach me the exercises. All my remonstrances were of no avail, he would frown and say:

"Father Moses, I can't stand it, that an honest man like you should know less than the rabble. Go along!"

And then we would up to the loft. It was very cold, but the sergeant was so provoked at my want of briskness in performing the movements, that he always put me in a great perspiration before we finished.

"Attention to the word of command, and no laziness!" he would exclaim.

I used to hear Sorlé, Safel, and the servant laughing in the stairway, as they peeped through the laths, and I did not dare to turn my head. In fine, it was entirely owing to this good Trubert that I learned to charge well, and became one of the best vaulters in the company.

Ah! Fritz, it would all have been very well if the spirits of wine had come; but instead of my dozen pipes, there came half a company of marine artillery, and four hundred recruits for the sixth light infantry.

About this time the governor ordered that a space

six hundred metres wide should be cleared all round the city.

You should have seen the havoc that was made in the place; the fences, palisades, and trees hewn down, the houses demolished, from which everybody carried away a beam or some timbers. You should have looked down from the ramparts and seen the little gardens, the line of poplars, the old trees in the orchards felled to the ground and dragged away by swarms of workmen. You should have seen all this to know what war is!

Father Frise, the two Camus boys, the Sades, the Bosserts, and all the families of the gardeners and small farmers who lived at Phalsburg, suffered the most. I can almost hear old Fritz exclaim:

"Ah! my poor apple-trees! Ah! my poor pear-trees; I planted you myself, forty years ago. How beautiful you were, always covered with fine fruit! Oh, misery! misery!"

And the soldiers still chopped away. Toward the end, old Fritz went away, his cap drawn over his eyes, and weeping bitterly.

The rumor spread also that they were going to burn the Maisons Rouges at the foot of the Mittlebronn hill, the tile-kiln at Pernette, and the little inns of *l'Arbre Vert* and *Panier Fleuri*, but it seemed that the governor found it was not necessary as these houses were out of range; or rather, that they would reserve that till later; and, that the allies were coming sooner than they were expected.

Of what happened before the blockade, I remember, too, that on the twenty-second of December, about eleven o'clock in the morning, the call was beat. Everybody supposed that it was for the drill, and I set out quietly, with my musket on my shoulder, as usual; but, as I reached the corner of the mayoralty, I saw the troops of the garrison formed under the trees of the square.

They placed us with them in two ranks; and then Governor Moulin, Commandants Thomas and Pettigenet, and the mayor, with his tri-colored sash, arrived.

They beat the march, and then the drum-major raised his baton, and the drums stopped. The governor began to speak, everybody listened, and the words heard from a distance were repeated from one to another.

"Officers, non-commissioned, National Guards, and Soldiers!

"The enemy is concentrated upon the Rhine, only three days' march from us. The city is declared to be in a state of siege; the civil authorities give place to martial law. A permanent court-martial replaces ordinary tribunals.

"Inhabitants of Phalsburg! we expect from you courage, devotion, obedience! *Vive l'Empereur!*"

And a thousand cries of "*Vive l'Empereur!*" filled the air.

I trembled to the ends of my hair; my spirits of wine were still on the road; I considered myself a ruined man.

The immediate distribution of cartridges, and the order to the battalion to go and forage for provisions, and bring in cattle from the surrounding villages for the supply of the city, prevented me from thinking of my misfortune.

I had also to think of my own life, for, in receiving such an order, we supposed of course that the peasants would resist, and it is abominable to have to fight the people you are robbing.

I was very pale as I thought of all this.

But when Commandant Thomas cried out, "Charge!" and I tore off my first cartridge, and put it in the barrel, and, instead of hearing the ramrod I felt a ball at the bottom!—when they orderd us: "By file—left! left! forward! quick step! march!" and we set out for the barracks of the Bois-de-Chênes, while the first battalion went on to Quatre-Vents and Bichelberg, the second to Wechern and Metting; when I thought that we were going to seize and carry away everything, and that the court-martial was at the mayoralty to pass sentence upon those who did not do their duty;—all these new and terrible things completely upset me. I was troubled as I saw the village in the distance, and pictured to myself beforehand the cries of the women and children.

You see, Fritz, to take from the poor peasant all his living at the beginning of winter; to take from him his cow, his goats, his pigs, everything in short, it is dreadful! and my own misfortune made me feel more for that of others.

And then, as we marched, I thought of my daughter Zeffen, and Baruch, and their children, and I exclaimed to myself:

"Mercy on us! if the enemy comes, what will they do in an exposed town like Saverne? They will lose everything. We may be beggared any day."

These thoughts took away my breath, and in the midst of them I saw some peasants, who, from their little windows, watched our approach over the fields and along their street, without stirring. They did not know what we were coming for.

Six mounted soldiers preceded us; Commandant Thomas ordered them to pass to the right and left of the barracks, to prevent the peasants from driving their cattle into the woods, when they had found out that we had come to rob them.

They set off on a gallop.

We came to the first house, where there is the stone crucifix. We heard the order:

"Halt!"

Then thirty men were detached to act as sentinels in the little streets, and I was among the number, which I liked, for I preferred being on duty to going into their stables and barns.

As we filed through the principal street the peasants asked us:

"What is going on? Have they been cutting wood? Have they been making arrests?" and such like questions. But we did not answer them, and hastened on.

Monborne placed me in the third street to the right, near the large house of Father Franz, who raised bees on the slope of the valley behind his house. We heard the sheep bleating and the cattle lowing; that wretch of a Monborne said, winking at me:

"It will be jolly! We will make the Baraquois open their eyes."

He had no mercy in him. He said to me:

"Moses, thou must stay there. If any one tries to pass, cross your bayonet. If any one resists, prick him well and then fire. The law must be supported by force."

I don't know where the cobbler picked up that expression; but he left me in the street, between two fences white with frost, and went on his way with the rest of the guard.

I waited there nearly twenty minutes, considering what I should do if the peasants tried to save their property, and thinking it would be much better to fire upon the cattle than upon their owners.

I was much perplexed and was very cold, when I heard a great shouting; at the same time the drum began to beat. Some men went into the stables and drove the cattle. The Baraquins swore and wept; some tried to defend themselves. Commandant Thomas cried out:

"To the square! Drive them to the square!"

Some cows escaped through the fences, and you can't imagine what a tumult there was. I congratulated myself that I was not in the midst of this pillage. But this did not last long, for suddenly a herd of goats, driven by two old women, filed down the street on their way to the valley.

Then I had to stop them with my bayonet and call out:

"Halt!"

One of the women, mother Migneron, knew me she had a pitchfork, and was very pale.

"Let me pass, Moses," said she.

I saw that she was coming slowly toward me, meaning to throw me down with her pitchfork. The other tried to drive the goats into a little garden at the side, but the slats were too near together, and the fence too high.

I should have liked to let them go by, and deny having seen anything; but, unfortunately, Lieutenant Rollet came up and called out:

"Attention!"

And two men of the company followed: Macry and Schweyer, the brewer.

Old Migneron, seeing me cross the bayonet, began to grind her teeth, saying:

"Ah! wretch of a Jew, thou'lt pay for this!"

She was so angry that she had no fear of my musket, and three times she tried to thrust her pitchfork into me; then I found the benefit of my drilling, for I parried all her attacks.

Two goats escaped between my legs; the rest were taken. The soldiers pushed back the old women, broke their pitchforks, and finally regained the chief street, which was full of cattle, lowing and kicking.

Old Migneron sat down on the fence and tore her hair.

Just then two cows came along, their tails in the air, leaping over the fences and upsetting everything, the baskets of bees and their old keeper Fortunately, as it was winter, the bees remained as if dead in their baskets, or else I believe they would have routed our whole battalion.

The horn of the *hardier**** sounded in the village. He had been summoned in the name of the law. This old *hardier*, Nickel, passed along the street, and the animals became quiet, and could be put in some order. I saw the procession go along the street; the oxen and cows in front, then the goats, and the pigs behind.

The Baraquins followed, flinging stones and throwing sticks. I saw that, if I should be forgotten, these wretches would fall upon me, and I should be murdered; but Sergeant Monborne, with other comrades, came and relieved me. They all laughed, and said:

"We have shaved them well! There is not a goat left at the Barracks; we have taken everything at one haul."

We hastened to rejoin the column, which marched in two lines at the right and left of the road, the cattle in the middle, our company behind, and Nickel, with Commandant Thomas, in front. This formed a file of at least three hundred paces. On

---

* Herdsman.

every animal a bundle of hay had been tied for fodder.

In this way we passed slowly into the cemetery lane.

Upon the glacis we halted, and tied up the animals, and the order came to take them down into the fosses behind the arsenal.

We were the first that returned; we had seized thirty oxen, forty-five cows, a quantity of goats and pigs, and some sheep.

All day long the companies were coming back with their booty, so that the fosses were filled with cattle, which remained in the open air. Then the governor said that the garrison had provisions for six months, and every inhabitant must prove that he had enough to last as long, and that domiciliary visits were to begin.

We broke ranks before the city hall. I was going up the main street, my gun on my shoulder, when some one called me:

"Hey! Father Moses!"

I turned and saw our sergeant.

"Well," said he, laughing, "you have made your first attack; you have brought us back some provisions. Well and good!"

"Yes, sergeant, but it is very sad!"

"What, sad? Thirty oxen, forty-five cows, some pigs and goats—it is magnificent!"

"To be sure, but if you had heard the cries of these poor people, if you had seen them!"

"Bah! bah!" said he. "*Primo*, Father Moses, soldiers must live; men must have their rations if they are going to fight. I have often seen these things done in Germany and Spain and Italy! Peasants are selfish; they want to keep their own; they do not regard the honor of the flag; that is trash! In some respects they would be worse than towns-people, if we were foolish enough to listen to them; we must be strict."

"We have been, sergeant," I replied; "but if I had been master, we should not have robbed these poor wretches; they are in a pitiable condition enough already."

"You are too compassionate, Father Moses, and you think that others are like yourself. But we must remember that peasants, citizens, civilians, live only by the soldiers, and have all the profit without wanting to pay any of the cost. If we followed your advice we should die of hunger in this little town; our peasants would support the Russians, the Austrians, and Bavarians at our expense. This pack of scoundrels would be having a good time from morning to night, and the rest of us would be as poor as church-mice. That would not do—there is no sense in it!"

He laughed aloud. We had now come into our passage, and I went up stairs.

"Is it thou, Moses?" asked Sorlé in the darkness, for it was nightfall.

"Yes, the sergeant and I."

"Ah, good!" said she; "I was expecting you."

"Madame Moses," exclaimed the sergeant, "your husband can boast now of being a real soldier; he has not yet seen fire, but he has charged with his bayonet."

"Ah!" said Sorlé, "I am very glad to see him back."

In the room, through the little white door-curtains, we saw the lamp burning, and smelt the soup. The sergeant went to his room, as usual, and we into ours. Sorlé looked at me with her great black eyes, she saw how pale I was, and knew what I was thinking about. She took from me my cartridge-box, and placed my musket in the closet.

"Where is Säfel?" I asked.

"He must be in the square. I sent him to see if you had come back. Hark! There he is coming up!"

Then I heard the child come up the stairs; he opened the door at once and ran joyfully to embrace me.

We sat down to dinner, and, in spite of my trouble, I ate with a good appetite, having taken nothing since morning.

Suddenly Sorlé said: "If the invoice does not come before the city gates are closed we shall not have to pay anything, for goods are at the risk of the merchant until they are delivered. And we have not received the inventory."

"Yes," I replied, "you are right; M. Quataya, instead of sending us the spirits of wine at once, waited a week before answering us. If he had sent the twelve pipes that day or the day after, they would be here by this time. The delay is not our fault."

You see, Fritz, how anxious we were; but, as the sergeant came to smoke his pipe at the corner of the stove, as usual, we said no more about it.

I spoke only of my fears in regard to Zeffen, Baruch, and their children, in an exposed town like Saverne. The sergeant tried to put my mind at ease, and said that in such places they made, to be sure, all sorts of requisitions in wines, brandies, provisions, carriages, carts, and horses, but, except in case of resistance, the people were let alone, and the soldiers even tried to keep on good terms with them.

We kept on talking till nearly ten o'clock; then

the sergeant, who had to keep guard at the German gate, went away, and we went to bed.

This was the night of the twenty-second and twenty-third of December, a very cold night.

IX.

APPROACH OF THE ENEMY.

The next morning, when I threw back the shutters of our room, everything was white with snow; the old elms of the square, the street, the roofs of the mayoralty and market and church. Some of our neighbors, Recco the tinman, Spick the baker, and old Durand the mattress-maker, opened their doors and looked as if dazzled, while they exclaimed:

"He! Winter has come!"

Although we see it every year yet it is like a new existence. We breathe better out of doors, and within it is a pleasure to sit in the corner of the fireplace and smoke our pipes, while we watch the crackling of the red fire. Yes, I have always felt so for seventy-five years, and I feel so still!

I had scarcely opened the shutters when Sâfel sprang from his bed like a squirrel, and came and flattened his nose against a pane of glass, his long hair dishevelled and his legs bare.

"Oh! snow! snow!" he exclaimed. "Now we can have some slides!"

Sorlé, in the next room, made haste to dress herself and run in. We all looked out for some minutes; then I went to make the fire, Sorlé went to the kitchen, Sâfel dressed himself hastily, and everything fell back into the ordinary channel.

Notwithstanding the falling snow, it was very cold. You need only to see the fire kindle at once, and hear it roar in the stove, to know that it was freezing hard.

As we were eating our soup, I said to Sorlé, "The poor sergeant must have passed a dreadful night. His little glass of cherry-brandy will taste good."

"Yes," she said, "it is well you thought of it."

She went to the closet, and filled my little pocket-flask from the bottle of cherry-brandy.

You know, Fritz, that **we** do not like to go into public houses when we are on our way to our own business. Each of us carries his own little bottle and crust of bread; it is the best way and most conformed to the law of the Lord.

Sorlé then filled my flask, and I put it in my pocket, under my great-coat, to go to the guard-house. Sâfel wanted to follow me, but his mother told him to stay, and I went down alone, well pleased at being able to do the sergeant a kindness.

It was about seven o'clock. The snow falling from the roofs at every gust of wind was enough to blind you. But going along the walls, with my nose in my great-coat, which was well drawn up on the shoulders, I reached the German gate, and was about going down the three steps of the guard-house, under the arch at the left, when the sergeant himself opened the heavy door and exclaimed:

"Is it you, Father Moses! What the devil has brought you here in this cold?"

The guard-house was full of mist; we could hardly see some men stretched on camp-beds at the further end, and five or six veterans near the red-hot stove.

I stood and looked.

"Here," I said to the sergeant as I handed him my little bottle, "I have brought you your drop of cherry-brandy; it was such a cold night, you must need it."

"And you have thought of me, Father Moses!" he exclaimed, taking me by the arm, and looking at me with emotion.

"Yes, sergeant."

"Well, I am glad of it."

He raised the flask to his mouth and took a good drink. At that moment there was a distant cry

"Who goes there?" and the guard of the outpost ran to open the gate.

"That is good!" said the sergeant, tapping on the cork, and giving me the bottle; "take it back, Father Moses, and thank you!"

Then he turned toward the half-moon and asked, "News! What is it?"

We both looked and saw a hussar quarter-master, a withered, gray old man, with quantities of chevrons on his arm, arrive in great haste.

All my life I shall have that man before my eyes; his smoking horse, his flying sabretash, his sword clinking against his boots; his cap and jacket covered with frost; his long, bony, wrinkled face, his pointed nose, long chin, and yellow eyes. I shall always see him riding like the wind, then stopping his rearing horse under the arch in front of us, and calling out to us with a voice like a trumpet: "Where is the governor's house, sergeant?"

"The first house at the right, quarter-master. What is the news?"

"The enemy is in Alsace!"

Those who have never seen such men—men accustomed to long warfare, and hard as iron—can have no idea of them. And then if you had heard the exclamation, "The enemy is in Alsace!" it would have made you tremble.

The veterans had gone away; the sergeant, as he saw the hussar fasten his horse at the governor's door, and said to me: "Ah, well, Father Moses, now we shall see the whites of their eyes!"

He laughed, and the others seemed pleased.

As for myself, I set forth quickly, with my head bent, and in my terror repeating to myself the words of the prophet:

"One post shall run to meet another, and one messenger to meet another, to show the king that his passages are stopped, and the reeds they have burned with fire, and the men of war are affrighted.

"The mighty men have forborne to fight, they have remained in their holds, their might hath failed, and the bars are broken.

"Set ye up a standard in the land, blow the trumpet among the nations, prepare the nations against her, call together against her the kingdoms, appoint a captain against her.

"And the land shall tremble and sorrow; for every purpose of the Lord shall be performed, to make the land a desolation without an inhabitant!"

I saw my ruin at hand—the destruction of my hopes.

"Mercy, Moses!" exclaimed my wife, as she saw me come back, "What is the matter? Your face is all drawn up. Something dreadful has happened."

"Yes, Sorlé," I said, as I sat down; "the time of trouble has come of which the prophet spoke: 'The king of the south shall push at him, and the king of the north shall come against him like a whirlwind: and he shall enter into the countries and shall overflow and pass over.'"

This I said with my hands raised toward heaven. Little Säfel squeezed himself between my knees, while Sorlé looked on, not knowing what to say; and I told them that the Austrians were in Alsace; that the Bavarians, Swedes, Prussians, and Russians were coming by hundreds of thousands; that a hussar had come to announce all these calamities; that our spirits of wine were lost, and ruin was threatening us.

I shed a few tears, and neither Sorlé nor Säfel would comfort me.

It was eight o'clock. There was a great commotion in the city. We heard the drum beat, and proclamations read; it seemed as if the enemy were already there.

One thing which I remember especially, for we had opened a window to hear, was that the governor ordered the inhabitants to empty immediately their barns and granaries; and that, while we were listening, a large Alsatian wagon with two horses, with Baruch sitting on the pole, and Zeffen behind on some straw—her infant in her arms, and her other child at her side—turned suddenly into the street.

They were coming to us for safety!

The sight of them upset me, and raising my hands, I exclaimed:

"Lord, take from me all weakness! Thou seest that I need to live for the sake of these little ones. Therefore be thou my strength, and let me not be cast down!"

And I went down at once to receive them, Sorlé and Säfel following me. I took my daughter in my arms, and helped her to the ground, while Sorlé took the children, and Baruch exclaimed:

"We came at the last minute! The gate was closed as soon as we had come in. There were many others from Quatre-Vents and Saverne who had to stay outside."

"God be praised, Baruch!" I replied. "You are all welcome, my dear children! I have not much, I am not rich; but what I have, you have—it is all yours. Come in!"

And we went up-stairs; Zeffen, Sorlé, and I carrying the children, while Baruch stayed to take their things out of the wagon, and then he came up.

The street was now full of straw and hay, thrown out from the lofts; there was no wind, and the snow had stopped falling. In a little while the shouts and proclamations ceased.

Sorlé hastened to serve up the remains of our breakfast, with a bottle of wine; and Baruch, while he was eating, told us that there was a panic in Alsace, that the Austrians had turned Basle, and were advancing by forced marches upon Schlestadt, Neuf Brisach, and Strasburg, after having surrounded Huninguen.

"Everybody is escaping," said he. "They are fleeing to the mountain, taking their valuables on their carts, and driving their cattle into the woods. There is a rumor already that bands of Cossacks have been seen at Mutzig, but that is hardly possible, as the army of Marshal Victor is on the Upper Rhine, and dragoons are passing every day to join him. How could they pass his lines without giving battle?"

We were listening very attentively to these things when the sergeant came in. He was just off duty, and stood outside of the door, looking at us with astonishment.

I took Zeffen by the hand, and said: "Sergeant, this is my daughter, this is my son-in-law, and these are my grandchildren, about whom I have told you. They know you, for I have told them in my letters how much we think of you."

The sergeant looked at Zeffen.—"Father Moses," said he, "you have a handsome daughter, and your son-in-law looks like a worthy man."

Then he took little Esdras from Zeffen's arms, and lifted him up, and made a face at him, at which the child laughed, and everybody was pleased. The other little one opened his eyes wide and looked on.

"My children have come to stay with me," I said to the sergeant; "you will excuse them if they make a little noise in the house?"

"How! Father Moses," he exclaimed. "I will excuse everything! Do not be concerned; are we not old friends?"

And at once, in spite of all we could say, he chose another room looking upon the court.

"All the nestful ought to be together," said he. "I am the friend of the family, the old sergeant, who will not trouble anybody, provided they are willing to see him here."

I was so much moved that I gave him both my hands.

"It was a happy day when you entered my house," said I. "The Lord be thanked for it!"

He laughed, and said: "Come now, Father Moses; come! Have I done anything more than was natural? Why do you wonder at it?"

He went at once to get his things and carry them

to his new room; and then went away, so as not to disturb us.

How we are mistaken! This sergeant, whom Frichard had sent to plague us, at the end of a fortnight was one of our family; he consulted our comfort in everything—and, notwithstanding all the years that have passed since then, I cannot think of that good man without emotion.

When we were alone, Baruch told us that he could not stay at Phalsburg; that he had come to bring his family, with everything that he could provide for them in the first hurried moments; but that, in the midst of such dangers, when the enemy could not long delay coming, his duty was to guard his house, and prevent, as much as possible, the pillage of his goods.

This seemed right, though it made us none the less grieved to have him go. We thought of the pain of living apart from each other; of hearing no tidings; of being all the time uncertain about the fate of our beloved ones! Meanwhile we were all busy. Sorlé and Zeffen prepared the children's bed; Baruch took out the provisions which he had brought; Sâfel played with the two little ones, and I went and came, thinking about our troubles.

At last, when the best room was ready for Zeffen and the children, as the German gate was already shut, and the French gate would be open only until two o'clock at the latest, for strangers to leave the city, Baruch exclaimed: "Zeffen, the moment has come!"

He had scarcely said the words when the great agony began—cries, embraces, and tears!

Ah! it is a great joy to be loved, the only true joy of life. But what sorrow to be separated! And how our family loved each other! How Zeffen and Baruch embraced one another! How they leaned over their little ones, how they looked at them, and began to sob again!

What can be said at such a moment? I sat by the window, with my hands before my face, without strength to speak. I thought to myself: "My God, must it be that a single man shall hold in his hands the fate of us all! Must it be that, for his pleasure, for the gratification of his pride, everything shall be confounded, overturned, torn asunder! My God, shall these troubles never end? Hast thou no pity on thy poor creatures?"

I did not raise my eyes, but I heard the lamentations which rent my heart, and which lasted till the moment when Baruch, perceiving that Zeffen was quite exhausted, ran out, exclaiming; "It must be! It must be! Adieu, Zeffen! Adieu, my children! Adieu, all!"

No one followed him.

We heard the carriage roll away, and then was the great sorrow—that sorrow of which it is written.

"By the rivers of Babylon, there we sat down; yea, we wept when we remembered Zion.

"We hanged our harps upon the willows.

"For there they that carried us away captive, required of us a song; saying: 'Sing us one of the songs of Zion!'

"How shall we sing the Lord's song in a strange land?"

X.

AN ENGAGEMENT WITH THE COSSACKS.

But that day I was to have the greatest fright of all. You remember, Fritz, that Sorlé had told me at supper the night before, that if we did not receive the invoice, our spirits of wine would be at the risk of M. Quataya of Pézenas, and that we need feel no anxiety about it.

I thought so, too, for it seemed to me right; and as the French and German gates were closed at three o'clock, and nothing more could enter the city, I supposed that that was the end of the matter, and felt quite relieved.

"It is a pity, Moses!" I said to myself, as I walked up and down the room; "yes, for if these spirits had been sent a week sooner, we should have made a great profit; but now, at least, thou art relieved of great anxiety. Be content with thine old trade. Let alone for the future such harassing undertakings.

Don't stake thine all again on one throw, and let this be a lesson to thee!"

Such thoughts were in my mind, when, about four o'clock, I heard some one coming up our stairs. It was a heavy step, as of a man trying to find his way in the dark.

Zeffen and Sorlé were in the kitchen, preparing supper. Women always have something to talk about by themselves, for nobody else to hear. So I listened, and then opened the door.

"Who is there?" I asked.

"Does not Mr. Moses, the wine-merchant, live here?" asked a man in a blouse and broad-brimmed felt hat, with his whip on his shoulder—a wagoner's figure, in short. I turned pale as I heard him, and replied: "Yes, my name is Moses. What do you want?"

He came in, and took out a large leather portfolio from under his blouse. I trembled as I looked on.

"There!" said he, giving me two papers, "my invoice and my bill of lading! Are not the twelve pipes of three-six from Pézenas for you?"

"Yes, where are they?"

"On the Mittelbronn hill, twenty minutes from here," he quietly answered. "Some Cossacks stopped my wagons, and I had to take off the horses. I hurried into the city by a postern under the bridge."

My legs failed me as he spoke. I sank into my arm-chair, unable to speak a word.

"You will pay me the portage," said the man, "and give me a receipt for the delivery."

"Sorlé! Sorlé!" I cried in a despairing voice And she and Zeffen ran to me. The wagoner explained it all to them. As for me, I heard nothing. I had strength only to exclaim: "Now all is lost! Now I must pay without receiving the goods."

"We are willing to pay, sir," said my wife, "but the letter states that the twelve pipes shall be delivered in the city."

The wagoner said: "I have just come from the justice of the peace, as I wanted to find out before coming to you what I had a right to claim; he told me that you ought to pay for everything, even my horses and carriages, do you understand? I unharnessed my horses, and escaped, myself, which is so much the less on your account. Will you settle? Yes or no?"

We were almost dead with fright when the sergeant came in. He had heard loud words, and asked: "What is it, Father Moses? What is it about? What does this man want?"

Sorlé, who never lost her presence of mind, told him the whole story, shortly and clearly; he comprehended it at once.

"Twelve pipes of three-six, that makes twenty four pipes of cognac. What luck for the garrison! what luck!"

"Yes," said I, "but it cannot come in; the city gates are shut, and the wagons are surrounded by Cossacks."

"Cannot come in!" cried the sergeant, raising his shoulders. "Go along! Do you take the governor for a fool? Is he going to refuse twenty-four pipes of good brandy, when the garrison needs it? Is he going to leave this windfall to the Cossacks? Madame Sorlé, pay the portage at once; and you, Father Moses, put on your cap and follow me to the governor's, with the letter in your pocket. Come along! Don't lose a minute! If the Cossacks have time to put their noses in your casks, you will find a famous deficit, I warrant you!"

When I heard that I exclaimed: "Sergeant, you have saved my life!" And I hastened to get my cap.

"Shall I pay the portage?" asked Sorlé.

"Yes! pay!" I answered as I went down, for it was plain that the wagoner could compel us. I went down with an anxious heart.

All that I remember after this is that the sergeant walked before me in the snow, that he said a few words to the sapper on orderly duty at the gov ernor's house, and that we went up the grand stairway with the marble balustrade.

Upstairs, in the gallery with the balustrade around it, he said to me: "Be easy, Father Moses! Take out your letter, and let me do the talking."

He knocked softly at a door as he spoke.

Somebody said: "Come in!"

We went in.

Colonel Moulin, a fat man in a dressing-gown and little silk cap, was smoking his pipe in front of a good fire. He was very red, and had a caraffe of rum and a glass at its side on the marble mantel-piece, where were also a clock and vases of flowers.

"What is it?" he asked, turning round.

"Colonel, this is what is the matter," replied the sergeant: "twelve pipes of spirits of wine have been stopped on the Mittelbronn hill, and are surrounded by Cossacks."

"Cossacks!" exclaimed the governor. "Have they broken through our lines already?"

"Yes," said the sergeant, "a sudden attack of Cossacks! They have possession of the twelve pipes of three-six which this patriot brought from Pézenas to sustain the garrison."

"Some bandits," said the governor—"thieves!"

"Here is the letter," said the sergeant, taking it from my hand.

The colonel cast his eyes over it, and said hastily:

"Sergeant, go and take twenty-five men of your company. Go on the run, free the wagons, and put in requisition horses from the village to bring them into the city."

And, as we were going: "Wait!" said he; and he went to his bureau and wrote four words; "here is the order."

When we were once on the stairway, the sergeant said: "Father Moses, run to the cooper's; we may perhaps need him and his boys. I know the Cossacks; their first thought will be to unload the casks so as to be more sure of keeping them. Have them bring ropes and ladders; and I will go to the Barracks and get my men together."

Then I ran home like a hart, for I was enraged at the Cossacks. I went in to get my musket and cartridge-box. I could have fought an army: I could not see straight.

"What is it? Where are you going?" asked Sorlé and Zeffen.

"You will know by-and-bye," I replied.

I went to Schweyer's. He had two large saddle-pistols, which he put quickly into his apron-belt with the axe; his two boys, Nickel and Frantz, took the ladder and ropes, and we ran to the French gate.

The sergeant was not yet there; but two minutes after he came running down the street by the rampart with thirty veterans in file, their muskets on their shoulders.

The officer guarding the postern had only to see the order to let us go out, and a few minutes after we were in the trenches behind the hospital, where the sergeant ranged his men.

"It is cognac!" he told them; "twenty-four pipes of cognac! So, comrades, attention! The garrison is without brandy; those who do not like brandy have only to fall to the rear."

But they all wanted to be in front, and laughed in anticipation.

We went up the stairway, and were ranged in order in the covered ways. It might have been five o'clock. Looking from the top of the glacis we could see the broad meadow of Eichmatt, and above it the hills of Mittelbronn covered with snow. The sky was full of clouds, and night was coming on. It was very cold.

"Forward!" said the sergeant.

And we gained the highway. The veterans ran, in two files, at the right and left, their backs rounded, and their muskets in their shoulder-belts; the snow was up to their knees.

Schweyer, his two boys, and I walked behind.

At the end of a quarter of an hour, the veterans, who ran all the way, had left us far behind; we heard for some time their cartridge-boxes rattling, but soon this sound was lost in the distance, and then we heard the dog of the Trois-Maisous barking in his chain.

The deep silence of the night gave me a chance to think. If it had not been for the thought of my spirits of wine, I would have gone straight back to Phalsburg, but fortunately that thought prevailed, and I said:

"Make haste, Schweyer, make haste!"

"Make haste!" he exclaimed angrily, "you can make haste to get back your spirits of wine, but what do we care for it? Is the highway the place for us? Are we bandits that we should risk our lives?"

I understood at once that he wanted to escape, and was enraged.

"Take care, Schweyer," said I, "take care! If you and your boys go back, people will say that you have been a traitor to the city brandy, and that is worse than being a traitor to the flag, especially in a cooper."

"The devil take thee!" said he, "we ought never to have come."

However, he kept on ascending the hill with me.

Nickel and Frantz followed us without hurrying.

When we reached the plateau we saw lights in the village. All was still and seemed quiet, although there was a great crowd around the two first houses.

The door of the *Bunch of Grapes* was wide open, and its kitchen fire shone through the passage to the street where my two wagons stood.

This crowd came from the Cossacks who were carousing at Heitz's house, after tying their horses under the shed. They had made Mother Heitz cook them a good hot soup, and we saw them plainly, two or three hundred paces distant, go up and down the outside steps, with jugs and bottles which they passed from one to another. The thought came to me that they were drinking my spirits of wine, for a lantern hung behind the first wagon, and the rascals were all going from it with their elbows raised. I was so furious that, regardless of danger, I began to run to put a stop to the pillage.

Fortunately the veterans were in advance of me, or I should have been murdered by the Cossacks; I had not gone half way when our whole troop sprang from the fences of the highway, and ran like a pack of wolves, crying out, "To the bayonet!"

You never saw such confusion, Fritz. In a second the Cossacks were on their horses, and the veterans in the midst of them; the front of the inn with its trellis, its pigeon-house, and its little fenced garden, was lighted up by the firing of muskets and pistols. Heitz's two daughters stood at the windows, with their arms lifted and screamed so that they could be heard all over Mittelbronn.

Every minute, in the midst of the confusion, something fell upon the road, and then the horses started and ran through the fields like deer, with their heads run out, and their manes and tails flying. The villagers ran; Father Heitz slipped into the barn, and climbed up the ladder, and I came up breathless, as if out of my senses.

I had not gone more than fifteen steps when a Cossack, who was running away at full speed, turned about furiously close to me, with his lance in the air, and called out, "Hurra!"

I had only time to stoop, and I felt the wind from the lance as it passed along my body.

I never felt so in my life, Fritz; I felt the chill of death, that trembling of the flesh, of which the prophet spoke: "Fear came upon me and trembling; the hair of my flesh stood up."

But what shows the spirit of wisdom and prudence which the Lord puts into his creatures, when he means to spare them for a good old age, is that immediately afterward, in spite of my trembling knees,

I went and sat under the first wagon, where the blows of the lances could not reach me; and there I saw the veterans finish the extermination of the rascals, who had retreated into the court, and not one of whom escaped.

Five or six were in a heap before the door, and three others were stretched upon the highway.

This did not take more than ten minutes; then all was dark again, and I heard the sergeant call: "Cease firing!"

Heitz, who had come down from his hay-loft, had just lighted a lantern; the sergeant seeing me under the wagon, called out: "Are you wounded, Father Moses?"

"No," I replied, "but a Cossack tried to thrust his lance into me, and I got into a safe place."

He laughed aloud, and gave me his hand to help me to rise.

"Father Moses," said he, "I was frightened about you. Wipe your back; people might think you were not brave."

I laughed too, and thought: "People may think what they please! The great thing is to live in good health as long as possible."

We had only one wounded, Corporal Duhem, an old man, who bandaged his own leg, and tried to walk. He had had a blow from a lance in the right calf. He was placed on the first wagon, and Lehnel, Heitz's granddaughter, came and gave him a drop of cherry-brandy, which at once restored his strength and even his good spirits.

"It is the fifteenth," he exclaimed. "I am in for a week at the hospital; but leave me the bottle for the compresses."

I was delighted to see my twelve pipes on the wagons, for Schweyer and his two boys had run away, and without their help we could hardly have reloaded.

I tapped at once at the bung-hole of the hindmost cask to find out how much was missing. Those scamps of Cossacks had already drunk nearly half a measure of spirits; Father Heitz told me that some of them scarcely added a drop of water. Such creatures must have throats of tin; the oldest topers among us could not bear a glass of three-six without being upset.

At last all was ready and we had only to return to the city. When I think of it, it all seems before me now: Heitz's large dapple-gray horses going out of the stable one by one; the sergeant standing by the dark door with his lantern in his hand, and calling out, "Come, hurry up! The rascals may come back!" On the road in front of the inn, the veterans surrounded the wagons; further on the right some peasants, who had hastened to the scene with pitchforks and mattocks, were looking at the dead Cossacks, and myself, standing on the stairs above, singing praises to God in my heart as I thought how glad Sorlé and Zeffen and little Sâfel would be to see me come back with our goods.

And then when all is ready, when the little bells jingle, when the whip snaps, and we start on the way—what delight!

Ah Fritz! everything looks bright after thirty years; we forget fears, anxieties, and fatigues; but the memory of good men and happy hours remains with us forever!

The veterans, on both sides of the wagons, with their muskets under their arms, escorted my twelve pipes as if they were the tabernacle: Heitz led the horses, and the sergeant and I walked behind.

"Well, Father Moses!" said he laughing, "it has all gone off well; are you satisfied?"

"More than I can possibly tell, sergeant! What would have been my ruin will make the fortune of my family, and we owe it all to you."

"Go along," said he, "you are joking."

He laughed, but I felt deeply; to have been in danger of losing everything, and then to regain it all and make profit out of it—it makes one feel deeply

I exclaimed inwardly: "I will praise thee, O Lord, among the people; and I will sing praises unto thee among the nations.

"For thy mercy is great above the heavens, and thy truth reacheth unto the clouds."

XI.

FATHER MOSES RETURNS IN TRIUMPH.

Now I must tell you about our return to Phalsburg.

You may suppose that my wife and children, after seeing me take my gun and go away, were in a state of great anxiety. About five o'clock Sorlé went out with Zeffen to try to learn what was going on, and only then they heard that I had started for Mittelbronn with a detachment of veterans.

Imagine their terror!

The rumor of these extraordinary proceedings had spread through the city, and quantities of people were on the bastion of the artillery barracks, looking on from the distance. Burguet was there, with the mayor, and other persons of distinction, and a number of women and children, all trying to see through the darkness. Some insisted that Moses marched with the detachment, but nobody would believe it, and Burguet exclaimed: "It is not possible that a sensible man like Moses would go and risk his life in fighting Cossacks—no, it is not possible!"

If I had been in his place I should have said the same of him. But what can you do, Fritz? The most prudent of men become blind when their property is at stake; blind, I say, and terrible, for they lose sight of danger.

This crowd was waiting, as I said, and soon Zeffen and Sorlé came, as pale as death, with their large shawls over their heads. They went up the rampart and stood there, with their feet in the snow, too much frightened to speak.

I learned these things afterward.

When Zeffen and her mother went up on the bastion, it was, perhaps, half-past five; there was not a star to be seen. Just at that time, Schweyer and his boys ran away, and five minutes later the skirmish began.

Burguet told me afterward that, notwithstanding the darkness and the distance, they saw the flash of the muskets around the inn as plainly as if they were a hundred paces off, and everybody was still and listened to hear the shots, which were repeated by the echoes of the Bois-de-chênes and Lutzelburg.

When they ceased Sorlé descended from the slope, leaning on Zeffen's arm, for she could not support herself. Burguet helped them to reach the street, and took them into old Frise's house on the corner, where they found him warming himself gloomily by his hearth.

"My last day has come!" said Sorlé. Zeffen wept bitterly.

I have often reproached myself for having caused this sorrow, but who can answer for his own wisdom? Has not the wise man himself said: "I turned myself to behold wisdom, and madness, and folly; and I saw that wisdom excelleth folly; and I myself perceived that one event happeneth to the wise man and the fool. Wherefore, I said in my heart, that wisdom also is vanity."

Burguet was going out from father Frise's when Schweyer and his sons came up the postern stairs, crying out that we were surrounded by Cossacks and lost. Fortunately my wife and daughter could not hear them, and the mayor soon came along and ordered them to stop talking and go home quickly, if they did not want to be sent to prison.

They obeyed, but that did not prevent people from believing what they said, especially as it was all dark again in the direction of Mittelbronn.

The crowd came down from the ramparts and

filled the street; many of them went to their homes thinking they should never see us again, when, just as the clock struck seven, the sentinel of the outworks called out, "Who goes there?"

We had reached the gate.

The crowd was soon on the ramparts again. The squad in front of the sergeant on duty flew to arms; they had just recognized us.

We heard the murmur, without knowing what it was. So, when, after a reconnoissance, the gates were slowly opened to us, and the two bridges lowered for us to pass, what was our surprise at hearing the shouts: "Hurrah for Father Moses!— Hurrah for the spirits of wine!"

The tears came to my eyes. And my wagons rolling heavily under the gates, the soldiers presented arms to us, the great crowd surrounding us, shouting: "Moses! Hey, Moses! are you all right? you have not been killed?" the shouts of laughter, the people seizing my arm to hear me tell about the fight,—all these things were very pleasant.

Everybody wanted to talk with me, even the mayor, and I had not time to answer them.

But all this was nothing compared with the joy I felt at seeing Sorlé, Zeffen, and little Säfel run from Father Frise's and throw themselves all at once into my arms, exclaiming: "He is safe! he is safe!"

Ah, Fritz! what are honors by the side of such love? What is all the glory of the world compared with the joy of seeing our beloved ones? The others might have cried out, "Hurrah for Moses!" a hundred years, and I would not even have turned my head; but I was terribly moved by the sight of my family.

I gave Sâfel my gun, and while the wagons, escorted by the veterans, went on toward the little market, I led Zeffen and Sorlé through the crowd to old Frise's, and there, when we were alone, we began to hug each other again.

Without, the shouts of joy were redoubled; you would have thought that the spirits of wine belonged to the whole city. But within the room, my wife and daughter burst into tears, and I confessed my imprudence.

So, instead of telling them of the dangers I had experienced, I told them that the Cossacks ran away as soon as they saw us, and that we had only to put horses to the wagons before starting.

A quarter of an hour afterward, when the cries and tumult had ceased, I went out, with Zeffen and Sorlé on my arms, and little Sâfel in front, with my gun on his shoulder, and in this way we went home, to see to the unlading of the brandy.

I wanted to put everything in order before morning, so as to begin to sell at double price as soon as possible.

When a man runs such risks he ought to make something by it; for if he should sell at cost price, as some persons wish, nobody would be willing to run any risk for the sake of others; and if it should come to pass that a man should sacrifice himself for other people, he would be thought a blockhead; we have seen it a hundred times, and it will always be so.

Thank God! such ideas never entered into my head! I have always thought that the true idea of trade was to make as much profit as we can, honestly and lawfully.

That is according to justice and good sense.

As we turned at the corner of the market, our two wagons were already unharnessed before our house. Heitz was running back with his horses, so as to take advantage of the open gates, and the veterans, with their arms at will, were going up the street toward the infantry quarters.

It might have been eight o'clock. Zeffen and Sorlé went to bed, and I sent Sâfel for Gros the cooper, to come and unload the casks. Quantities of people came and offered to help us. Gros came soon with his boys, and the work began.

It is very pleasant, Fritz, to see great tuns going

into your cellar, and to say to yourself, "These splendid tuns are mine: it is spirits which cost me twenty sous the quart, and which I am going to sell for three francs!" This shows the beauty of trade; but everybody can imagine the pleasure for himself—there is no use in speaking of it.

About midnight my twelve pipes were down on the stands, and there was nothing left to do but to broach them.

While the crowd was dispersing, I engaged Gros to come in the morning to help me mix the spirits with water, and we went up, well pleased with our day's work. We closed the double oak door, and I fastened the padlock and went to bed.

What a pleasure it is to own something and feel that it is all safe!

This is how my twelve pipes were saved.

You see now, Fritz, what anxieties and fears we had at that time. Nobody was sure of anything; for you must not suppose that I was the only one living like a bird on the branch; there were hundreds of others who were not able to close their eyes. You should have seen how the citizens looked every morning, when they heard that the Austrians and Russians occupied Alsace, that the Prussians were marching upon Sarrebruck, or when an order was published for domiciliary visits, or for days' labor to wall up the posterns and orillons of the place, or to form companies of firemen to remove at once all inflammable matter, or to report to the governor the situation of the city treasury, and the list of the principal persons subject to taxes for the supply of shoes, caps, bed-linen, and so forth.

You should have seen how people looked at each other.

In war times civil life is nothing, and they will take from you your last shirt, giving you the governor's receipt for it. The first men of the land are zeros when the governor has spoken. This is why I have often thought that everybody who wishes for war, or at least wants to be a soldier, is either demented or half ruined, and hopes to better himself by the ruin of everybody else. It must be so.

But notwithstanding all these troubles, I could not lose time, and I spent all the next day in mixing my spirits. I took off my cloak, and drew out with great gusto. Gros and his boys brought jugs, and emptied them in the casks which I had bought beforehand, so that by evening these casks were brimful of good white brandy, eighteen degrees.

I had caramel prepared, also, to give the brandy a good color of old cognac, and when I turned the faucet, and raised the glass before the candle, and saw that it was exactly the right tint, I was in ecstacies, and exclaimed: "Give strong drink unto him that is ready to perish, and wine unto those that be of heavy hearts! Let him drink and remember his misery no more."

Father Gros, standing at my side on his great flat feet, smiled quietly, and his boys looked well pleased.

I filled the glass for them; they passed it to each other and were delighted with it.

About five o'clock we went upstairs. Säfel, on the same day, had brought three workmen, and had them remove our old iron into the court under the shed. The old rickety storehouse was cleaned. Desmarets, the joiner, put up some shelves behind the door in the arch, for holding bottles, and glasses, and tin measures, when the time for selling should come, and his son put together the planks of the counter. This was all done at once, as at a time of great pressure, when people like to make a good sum of money quickly.

I looked at it all with a good deal of satisfaction. Zeffen, with her baby in her arms, and Sorlé, had also come down. I showed my wife the place behind the counter, and said, "That is the place where you are to sit, with your feet in loose slippers, and a warm tippet on your shoulders, and sell our brandy."

She smiled as she thought of it.

Our neighbors, Bailly the armorer, Koffel the little

weaver, and several others, came and looked on without speaking; they were astonished to see what quick work we were making.

At six o'clock, just as Desmarets laid aside his hammer, the sergeant arrived in great glee, on his return from the cantine.

"Well, Father Moses!" he exclaimed, "the work goes on! But there is still something wanting."

"What is that, sergeant?"

"Hi! It is all right, only you must put a screen up above, or look out for the shells!"

I saw that he was right, and we were all well frightened, except the neighbors, who laughed to see our surprise.

"Yes," said the sergeant, "we must have it."

This took away all my pleasure; I saw that our troubles were not yet at an end.

Sorlé, Zeffen, and I went up, while Desmarets closed the door. Supper was ready; we sat down thoughtfully, and little Sâfel brought the keys.

The noise had ceased without; now and then a citizen on patrol passed by.

The sergeant came to smoke his pipe as usual. He explained how the screens were made, by crossing beams in the form of a sentry-box, the two sides supported against the gables, but while he maintained that it would hold like an arch, I did not think it strong enough, and I saw by Sorlé's face that she thought as I did.

We sat there talking till ten o'clock, and then all went to bed.

XII.

THE ENEMY REPULSED.

About one o'clock in the morning of the sixth of January, the day of the feast of the Kings, the enemy arrived on the hill of Saverne.

It was terribly cold, our windows under the persiennes were white with frost. I woke as the clock struck one; they were beating the call at the infantry barracks.

You can have no idea how it sounded in the silence of the night.

"Dost thou hear, Moses?" whispered Sorlé.

"Yes, I hear," said I, almost without breathing.

After a minute some windows were opened in our street, and we knew that others too were listening; then we heard running, and suddenly the cry, "To arms! to arms!"

It made one's hair stand on end.

I had just risen, and was lighting a lamp, when we heard two knocks at our door.

"Come in!" said Sorlé, trembling.

The sergeant opened the door. He was in marching equipments, with his gaiters on his legs, his large gray cap turned up at the sides, his musket on his shoulder, and his sabre and cartridge-box on his back.

"Father Moses," said he, "go back to bed and be quiet: it is the battalion call at the barracks, and has nothing to do with you."

And we saw at once that he was right, for the drums did not come up the street two by two, as when the national guard was called in.

"Thank you, sergeant." I said.

"Go to sleep!" said he, and he went down the stairs.

The door of the alley below slammed to. Then the children, who had waked up, began to cry. Zeffen came in, very pale, with her baby in her arms, exclaiming, "Mercy! What is the matter?"

"It is nothing, Zeffen," said Sorlé. "It is nothing, my child: they are beating the call for the soldiers."

At the same moment the battalion came down the main street. We heard them march as far as to the Place d'Armes, and beyond it toward the German gate.

We shut the windows, Zeffen went back to her room, and I lay down again.

But how could I sleep after such a start? My head was full of a thousand thoughts: I fancied the arrival of the Russians on the hill this cold night, and our soldiers marching to meet them, or manning the ramparts. I thought of all the blindages and block-houses, and batteries inside the bastions, and that all these great works had been made to guard against bombs and shells, and I exclaimed inwardly: "Before the enemy has demolished all these works, our houses will be crushed, and we shall be exterminated to the last man."

I took on in this way for about half an hour, thinking of all the calamities which threatened us, when I heard outside the city, toward Quatre-Vents, a kind of heavy rolling, rising and falling like the murmur of running water. This was repeated every second. I raised myself on my elbow to listen, and I knew that it was a fight far more terrible than that at Mittelbronn, for the rolling did not stop, but seemed rather to increase.

"How they are fighting, Sorlé, how they are fighting!" I exclaimed, as I pictured to myself the fury of those men murdering each other at the dead of night, not knowing what they were doing. "Listen! Sorlé, listen! If that does not make one shudder!"

"Yes," said she. "I hope our sergeant will not be wounded; I hope he will come back safe!"

"May the Lord watch over him!" I replied, jumping from my bed, and lighting a candle.

I could not control myself. I dressed myself as quickly as if I were going to run away; and afterward I listened to that terrible rolling, which came nearer or died away with every gust of wind.

When once dressed, I opened a window, to try to see something. The street was still black; but toward the ramparts, above the dark line of the arsenal bastions, was stretched a line of red.

The smoke of powder is red on account of the musket shots which light it up. It looked like a great fire. All the windows in the street were open: nothing could be seen, but I heard our neighbor the armorer say to his wife, "It is growing warm down there! It is the beginning of the dance, Annette; but they have not got the big drum yet; that will come, by and by!"

The woman did not answer, and I thought, "Is it possible to jest about such things! It is against nature."

The cold was so severe that after five or six minutes I shut the window. Sorlé got up and made a fire in the stove.

The whole city was in commotion; men were

shouting and dogs barking. Säfel, who had been wakened by all these noises, went to dress himself in the warm room. I looked very tenderly on this poor little one, his eyes still heavy with sleep; and as I thought that we were to be fired upon, that we must hide ourselves in cellars, and all of us be in danger of being killed for matters which did not concern us, and about which nobody had asked our opinion, I was full of indignation. But what distressed me most was to hear Zeffen sob and say that it would have been better for her and her children to stay with Baruch at Saverne and all die together.

Then the words of the prophet came to me: "Is not this thy fear, thy confidence, thy hope, and the uprightness of thy ways?

"Remember, I pray thee, who ever perished being innocent, or where were the righteous cut off.

"No, they that plow iniquity and sow wickedness, reap the same.

"By the blast of God they perish, and by the breath of his nostrils are they consumed.

"But thee, his servant, he shall redeem from death.

"Thou shalt come to thy grave in a full age, like as a shock of corn cometh in his season."

In this way I strengthened my heart, while I heard the great tumult of the panic-stricken crowd, running and trying to save their property.

About seven o'clock it was announced that the casemates were open, and that everybody might take their mattresses there, and that there must be tubs full of water in every house, and the wells left open in case of fire.

Think, Fritz, what ideas these orders suggested.

Some of our neighbors, Lisbeth Dubourg, Bével Ruppert, Camus' daughters, and some others, came up to us exclaiming, "We are all lost!"

Their husbands had gone out, right and left, to see what they could see, and these women hung on Zeffen and Sorlé's necks, repeating again and again, "Oh, dear! oh, dear! what misery!"

I could have wished them all to the devil, for instead of comforting us they only increased our fears; but at such times women will get together and cry out all at once; you can't talk reason to them; they like these loud cryings and groanings.

Just as the clock struck eight, Bailly the armorer came to find his wife: he had come from the ramparts. "The Russians," he said, "have come down in a mass from Quatre-Vents to the very gate, filling the whole plain—Cossacks, Baskirs, and rabble! Why don't they fire down upon them from the ramparts? The governor is betraying us."

"Where are our soldiers?" I asked.

"Retreating!" exclaimed he. "The wounded

came back two hours ago, and our men stay yonder, with folded arms."

His bony face shook with rage. He led away his wife; then others came crying out. "The enemy has advanced to the lower part of the gardens, upon the glacis." I was astonished at these things.

The women had gone away to cry somewhere else, and just then a great noise of wheels was heard from the direction of the rampart. I looked out of the window, and saw a wagon from the arsenal, some citizen gunners; old Goulden, Holender, Jacob Cloutier, and Barrier galloped at its sides; Captain Jovis ran in front. They stopped at our door.

"Call the iron-merchant!" cried the captain. "Tell him to come down."

Baker Chanoine, the brigadier of the second battery, came up. I opened the door.

"What do you want of me?" I asked in the stairway.

"Come down, Moses," said Chanoine. And I went down.

Captain Jovis, a tall old man, with his face covered with sweat, in spite of the cold, said to me, "You are Moses, the iron-merchant?"

"Yes, sir."

"Open your storehouse. Your iron is required for the defence of the city."

So I had to lead all these people into my court, under the shed. The captain on looking round, saw some cast-iron bars, which were used at that time for closing up the backs of fire-places. They weighed from thirty to forty pounds each, and I sold a good many in the vicinity of the city. There was no lack of old nails, rusty bolts, and old iron of all sorts.

"This is what we want," said he. "Break up these bars, and take away the old iron, quick!"

The others, with the help of our two axes, began at once to break up everything. Some of them filled a basket with the pieces of cast-iron, and ran with it to the wagon.

The captain looked at his watch, and said, "Make haste! We have just ten minutes!"

I thought to myself, "They have no need of credit; they take what they please; it is more convenient."

All my bars and old iron were broken in pieces—more than fifteen hundred pounds of iron.

As they were starting to run to the ramparts, Chanoine laughed, and said to me, "Capital grape-shot, Moses! Thou canst get ready thy pennies. We'll come and take them to-morrow."

The wagon started through the crowd which ran behind it, and I followed too.

As we came nearer the ramparts the firing became more and more frequent. As we turned from the curate's house two sentinels stopped everybody, but they let me pass on account of my iron, which they were going to fire.

You can never imagine that mass of people, the noise around the bastion, the smoke which covered it, the orders of the infantry officers whom we heard going up the glacis, the gunners, the lighted match, caissons with the piles of bullets behind! No, in all these thirty years I have not forgotten those men with their levers, running back the cannon to load them to their mouths; those firings in file, at the bottom of the ramparts; those volleys of balls hissing in the air; the orders of the gun-captains, "Load! Ram! Prime!"

What crowds upon those gun-carriages, seven feet high, where the gunners were obliged to stand and stretch their arms to fire the cannon! And what a frightful smoke!

Men invent such machines to destroy each other, and they would think that they did a great deal if they sacrificed a quarter as much to assist their fellow-men, to instruct them in infancy, and to give them a little bread in their old age.

Ah! those who make an outcry against war, and demand a different state of things, are not in the wrong.

I was in the corner, at the left of the bastion,

where the stairs go down to the postern behind the college, among three or four willow baskets as high as chimneys, and filled with clay. I ought to have stayed there quietly, and made use of the right moment to get away, but the thought seized me that I would go and see what was going on below the ramparts, and while they were loading the cannon, I climbed to the level of the glacis, and lay down flat between two enormous baskets, where there was scarcely a chance that balls could reach me.

If hundreds of others who were killed in the bastions had done as I did, how many of them might be still living, respectable fathers of families in their villages!

Lying in this place, and raising my nose, I could see over the whole plain. I saw the cordon of the rampart below, and the line of our skirmishers behind the palankas, on the other side of the moat; they did nothing but tear off their cartridges, prime, charge, and fire. There one could appreciate the beauty of drilling; there were only two companies of them, and their firing by file kept up an incessant roll.

Further on, directly to the right, stretched the road to Quatre-Vents. The Ozillo farm, the cemetery, the horse-post-station, and George Mouton's farm at the right; the inn of La Roulette and the great poplar-walk at the left, all were full of Cossacks, and such like rascals, who were gallopping into the very gardens, to reconnoitre the environs of the place. This is what I suppose, for it is against nature to run without an object, and to risk being struck by a ball.

These people, mounted on small horses, with large gray cloaks, soft boots, fox-skin caps, like those of the Baden peasants, long beards, lances in rest, great pistols in their belts, came whirling on like birds.

They had not been fired upon as yet, because they kept themselves scattered, so that bullets would have no effect; but their trumpets sounded the rally from La Roulette, and they began to collect behind the buildings of the inn.

About thirty of our veterans, who had been kept back in the cemetery lane, were making a slow retreat; they made a few paces, at the same time hastily reloading, then turned, shouldered, fired, and began marching again among the hedges and bushes, which there had not been time to cut down in this locality.

Our sergeant was one of these; I recognized him at once, and trembled for him.

Every time these veterans gave fire, five or six

Cossacks came on like the wind, with their lances lowered; but it did not frighten them: they leaned against a tree and levelled their bayonets. Other veterans came up, and then some loaded, while others parried the blows. Scarcely had they torn open their cartridges when the Cossacks fled right and left, their lances in the air. Some of them turned for a moment and fired their large pistols behind like regular bandits. At length our men began to march toward the city.

Those old soldiers, with their great shakos set square on their heads, their large capes hanging to the back of their calves, their sabres and cartridge-boxes on their backs, calm in the midst of these savages, reloading, trimming, and parrying as quietly as if they were smoking their pipes in the guard-house, were something to be admired. At last, after seeing them come out of the whirlwind two or three times, it seemed almost an easy thing to do.

Our sergeant commanded them. I understood then why he was such a favorite with the officers, and why they always took his part against the citizens; there were not many such. I wanted to call out, "Make haste, sergeant; let us make haste!" but neither he nor his men hurried in the least.

As they reached the foot of the glacis, suddenly a

large mass of Cossacks, seeing that they were escaping, galloped up in two files, to cut off their retreat It was the dangerous moment, and they formed in a square instantly.

I felt my back turn cold, as if I had been one of them.

Our sharpshooters behind the ammunition wagons did not fire, doubtless for fear of hitting their comrades; our gunners on the bastion leaned down to see, and the file of Cossacks stretched to the corner near the drawbridge.

There were seven or eight hundred of them. We heard them cry, "Hurra! hurra! hurra!" like crows. Several officers in green cloaks and small caps galloped at the sides of their lines, with raised sabres. I thought our poor sergeant and his thirty men were lost; I thought already, "How sorry little Säfel and Sorlé will be!"

But then, as the Cossacks formed in a half circle at the left of the outworks, I heard our gun-captain call out, "Fire!"

I turned my head; old Goulden struck the match, the fusee glittered, and at the same instant the bastion with its great baskets of clay shook to the very rocks of the rampart.

I looked toward the road; nothing was to be seen but men and horses on the ground.

Just then came a second shot, and I can truly say that I saw the grapeshot pass like the stroke of a scythe into that mass of cavalry; it all tumbled and fell; those who a second before were living beings were now nothing. We saw some try to raise themselves, the rest made their escape.

The firing by file began again, and our gunners, without waiting for the smoke to clear away, reloaded so quickly that the two discharges seemed to come at once.

This mass of old nails, bolts, broken bits of cast-iron, flying three hundred metres, almost to the little bridge, made such slaughter that, some days after, the Russians asked for an armistice in order to bury their dead.

Four hundred were found scattered in the ditches of the road.

This I saw myself.

And if you want to see the place where those savages were buried, you have only to go up the cemetery lane.

On the other side, at the right, in M. Adam Ottendorf's orchard, you will see a stone cross in the middle of the fence; they were all buried there, with their horses, in one great trench.

You can imagine the delight of our gunners at

seeing this massacre. They lifted up their sponges and shouted, "Vive i'Empereur!"

The soldiers shouted back from the covered ways, and the air was filled with their cries.

Our sergeant, with his thirty men, their guns on their shoulders, quietly reached the glacis. The barrier was quickly opened for them, but the two companies descended together to the moat and came up again by the postern.

I was waiting for them above.

When our sergeant came up I took him by the arm, "Ah, sergeant!" said I, "how glad I am to see you out of danger!"

I wanted to embrace him. He laughed and squeezed my hand.

"Then you saw the engagement, Father Moses!" said he, with a mischievous wink. "We have shown them what stuff the Fifth is made of!"

"Oh, yes! yes! you have made me tremble."

"Bah!" said he, "you will see a good deal more of it; it is a small affair."

The two companies reformed against the wall of the chemin de ronde, and the whole city shouted, "Vive l'Empereur!"

They went down the rampart street in the midst of the crowd. I kept near our sergeant.

As the detachment was turning our corner, Sorlé

Zeffen, and Sâfel called out from the windows. "Hurrah for the veterans! Hurrah for the Fifth!"

The sergeant saw them and made a little sign to them with his head. As I was going in I said to him, "Sergeant, don't forget your glass of cherry-brandy."

"Don't worry, Father Moses," said he.

The detachment went on to break ranks at the Place d'Armes as usual, and I went up home at a quarter to four. I was scarcely in the room before Zeffen, Sorlé, and Sâfel threw their arms round me as if I had come back from the war; little David clung to my knee, and they all wanted to know the news.

I had to tell them about the attack, the grape-shot, the routing of the Cossacks. But the table was ready. I had not had my breakfast, and I said, "Let us sit down. You shall hear the rest by-and-bye. Let me take breath."

Just then the sergeant entered in fine spirits, and set the butt-end of his musket on the floor. We were going to meet him when we saw a tuft of red hair on the point of his bayonet, that made us tremble.

"Mercy, what is that?" said Zeffen, covering her face.

He knew nothing about it, and looked to see, much surprised.

"That?" said he, "Oh! it is the beard of a Cossack that I touched as I passed him—it is not much of anything."

He took the musket at once to his own room; but we were all horror-struck, and Zeffen could not recover herself. When the sergeant came back she was still sitting in the arm-chair, with both hands before her face.

"Ah, Madame Zeffen," said he sadly, "now you are going to detest me!"

I thought, too, that Zeffen would be afraid of him, but women always like these men who risk their lives at random. I have seen it a hundred times. And Zeffen smiled as she answered: "No, sergeant, no; these Cossacks ought to stay at home and not come and trouble us! You protect us—we love you very much!"

I persuaded him to breakfast with us, and it ended by his opening a window, and calling out to some soldiers passing by to give notice at the cantine that Sergeant Trubert was not coming to breakfast.

So we were all calmed down, and seated ourselves at the table. Sorlé went down to get a bottle of good wine, and we began to eat our breakfast.

We had coffee, too, and Zeffen wanted to pour it out herself for the sergeant. He was delighted.

"Madame Zeffen," said he, "you load me with kindness!"

She laughed. We had never been happier.

While he was taking his cherry-brandy, the sergeant told us all about the attack in the night; the way in which the Wurtemberg troops had stationed themselves at La Roulette, how it had been necessary to dislodge them as they were forcing open the two large gates, the arrival of the Cossacks at daybreak, and the sending out two companies to fire at them.

He told all this so well that we could almost think we saw it. But about eleven o'clock, as I took up the bottle to pour out another glassful, he wiped his mustache, and said, as he rose: "No, Father Moses, we have something to do besides taking our ease and enjoying ourselves; to-morrow, or next day, the shells will be coming; it is time to go and screen the garret."

We all became sober at these words.

"Let us see!" said he; "I have seen in your court some long logs of wood which have not been sawed, and there are three or four large beams against the wall. Are we two strong enough to carry them up? Let us try!"

He was going to take off his cape at once; but, as the beams were very heavy, I told him to wait and I would run for the two Carabins, Nicolas, who was called the *Greyhound*, and Mathis, the wood-sawyer. They came at once, and, being used to heavy work, they carried up the timber. They had brought their saws and axes with them; the sergeant made them saw the beams, so as to cross them above in the form of a sentry-box. He worked himself like a regular carpenter, and Sorlé, Zeffen, and I looked on. As it took some time, my wife and daughter went down to prepare supper, and I went down with them, to get a lantern for the workmen.

I was going up again very quietly, never thinking of danger, when, suddenly, a frightful noise, a kind of terrible rumbling, passed along the roof, and almost made me drop my lantern.

The two Carabins turned pale and looked at each other.

"It is a ball!" said the sergeant.

At the same time a loud sound of cannon in the distance was heard in the darkness.

I had a terrible feeling in my stomach, and I thought to myself, "Since one ball has passed, there may be two, three, four!"

My strength was all gone. The two Carabins doubtless thought the same, for they took down at once their waistcoats, which were hanging on the gable, to go away.

"Wait!" said the sergeant. "It is nothing Let us keep at our work—it is going on well. It will be done in an hour more."

But the elder Carabin called out, "You may do as you please! *I* am not going to stay here—I have a family!"

And while he was speaking, a second ball, more frightful than the first, began to rumble upon the roof, and five or six seconds after we heard the explosion.

It was astonishing! The Russians were firing from the edge of the Bois-de-Chênes, more than a half-hour distant, and yet we saw the red flash pass before our two windows, and even under the tiles.

The sergeant tried to keep us still at work.

"Two bullets never pass in the same place," said he. "We are in a safe spot, since that has grazed the roof. Come, let us go to work!"

It was too much for us. I placed the lantern on the floor and went down, feeling as if my thighs were broken. I wanted to sit down at every step.

Out of doors they were shouting as if it were morning, and in a more frightful way. Chimneys were falling, and women running to the windows; but I paid no attention to it, I was so frightened myself.

The two Carabins had gone away paler than death.

All that night I was ill. Sorlé and Zeffen were no more at ease than myself. The sergeant kept on alone, placing the logs and making them fast. About midnight he came down.

"Father Moses," said he, "the roof is screened, but your two men are cowards; they left me alone."

I thanked him, and told him that we were all sick, and as for myself I had never felt anything like it. He laughed.

"I know what that is," said he. "Conscripts always feel so when they hear the first ball; but that is soon over—they only need to get a little used to it."

Then he went to bed, and everybody in the house, except myself, went to sleep.

The Russians did not fire after ten o'clock that night; they had only tried one or two field-pieces, to warn us of what they had in store.

All this, Fritz, was but the beginning of the blockade; you are going to hear now of the miseries we endured for three months.

XIII.

A DESERTER CAPTURED.

The city was joyful the next day, notwithstanding the firing in the night. A number of men who came from the ramparts about seven o'clock, came down our street shouting: "They are gone! There is not a single Cossack to be seen in the direction of Quatre-Vents, nor behind the barracks of the Bois-de-Chênes! *Vive l'Empereur!*"

Everybody ran to the bastions.

I had opened one of our windows, and leaned out in my nightcap. It was thawing, the snow was sliding from the roofs, and that in the streets was melting in the mud. Sorlé, who was turning up our bed, called to me: "Do shut the window, Moses! We shall catch cold from the draught!"

But I did not listen. I laughed as I thought: "The rascals have had enough of my old bars and rusty nails; they have found out that they fly a good way: experience is a good thing!"

I could have stayed there till night to hear the neighbors talk about the clearing away of the Russians, and those who came from the ramparts declaring that there was not one to be seen in the whole region. Some said that they might come back, but that seemed to me contrary to reason. It was clear that the villains would not quit the country at once, that they would still for a long time pillage the villages, and live on the peasants; but to believe that the officers would excite their men to take our city, or that the soldiers would be foolish enough to obey them, never entered my head.

At last Zeffen came into our room to dress the children, and I shut the window. A good fire roared in the stove. Sorlé made ready our breakfast, while Zeffen washed her little Esdras in a basin of warm water.

"Ah, now, if I could only hear from Baruch, it would all be well," said she.

Little David played on the floor with Sâfel, and I thanked the Lord for having delivered us from the scoundrels.

While we were at breakfast, I said to my wife: "It has all gone well! We shall be shut up for a while until the Emperor has carried the day, but they will not fire upon us, they will be satisfied with blockading us; and bread, wine, meats, and brandies, will grow dearer. It is the right time for us to sell, or else we might fare like the people of Samaria when Ben-Hadad besieged their city. There was a great famine, so that the head of an ass sold for four-score pieces of silver, and the fourth part of a cab of dove's-dung for five pieces. It was a good price; but still the merchants were holding back, when a noise of chariots and horses and of a great host came from heaven, and made the Syrians escape with Ben-Hadad, and after the people had pillaged their camp, a measure of fine flour sold for only a shekel, and two measures of barley for a shekel. So let us try to sell while things are at a reasonable price; we must begin in good season."

Sorlé assented, and after breakfast I went down to the cellar to go on with the mixing.

Many of the mechanics had gone back to their work. Klipfel's hammer sounded on his anvil. Chanoine put back his rolls into his windows, and Tribolin, the druggist, his bottles of red and blue water behind his panes.

Confidence was restored everywhere. The citizen-gunners had taken off their uniforms, and the joiners had come back to finish our counter; the noise of the saw and plane filled the house.

Everybody was glad to return to his own business,

for war brings nothing but harm; the sooner it is over the better.

As I carried my jugs from one tun to another, in the cellar, I saw the passers-by stop before our old shop, and heard them say to each other, "Moses is going to make his fortune with the brandy; these rascals of Jews always have good scent; while we have been selling this month past, he has been buying. Now that we are shut up he can sell at any price he pleases."

You can judge whether that was not pleasant to hear! A man's greatest happiness is to succeed in his business; everybody is obliged to say: "This man has neither army, nor generals, nor cannon, he has nothing but his own wit, like everybody else; when he succeeds he owes it to himself, and not to the courage of others. And then he ruins no one; he does not rob, or steal, or kill; while, in war, the strongest crushes the weakest and often the best."

So I worked on with great zeal, and would have kept on till night if little Säfel had not come to call me to dinner. I was hungry, and was going up-stairs, glad in the thought of sitting down in the midst of my children, when the call-beat began on the Place d'Armes, before the town-house. During a blockade a court-martial sits continually at the mayoralty to try those who do not answer to the call. Some of my neighbors were already leaving their houses with their muskets on their shoulders. I had to go up very hastily, and swallow a little soup, a morsel of meat, and a glass of wine.

I was very pale. Sorlé, Zeffen, and the children said not a word. The drum corps continued the call to arms; it came down the main street and stopped at last before our house, on the little square. Then I ran for my cartridge-box and musket.

"Ah!" said Sorlé, "we thought we were going to have a quiet time, and now it is all beginning again."

Zeffen did not speak, but burst into tears.

At that moment the old rabbi Heymann came in, with his old martin-skin cap drawn down to the nape of his neck.

"For heaven's sake let the women and children hurry to the casements! An envoy has come threatening to burn the whole city if the gates are not opened. Fly, Sorlé! Zeffen, fly!"

Imagine the cries of the women on hearing this; as for myself, my hair stood on end.

"The rascals have no shame in them!" I exclaimed! "They have no pity on women or children! May the curse of heaven fall on them!"

Zeffen threw herself into my arms. I did not know what to do.

But the old rabbi said: "They are doing to us what our people have done to them! So the words of the Lord are fulfilled: 'As thou hast done unto thy brother so shall it be done unto thee!'—But, you must fly quickly."

Below, the call-beat had ceased; my knees trembled. Sorlé, who never lost courage, said to me: "Moses, run to the square, make haste, or they will send you to prison!"

Her judgment was always right; she pushed me by the shoulders, and in spite of Zeffen's tears I went down, calling out: "Rabbi, I trust in you—save them!"

I could not see clearly; I went through the snow, miserable man that I was, running to the town-house where the national guard was already assembled. I came just in time to answer the call, and you can imagine my trouble, for Zeffen, Sorlé, Säfel, and the little ones were abandoned before my eyes. What was Phalsburg to me? I would have opened the gates in a minute to have had peace.

The others did not look any better pleased than myself; they were all thinking of their families.

Our governor, Moulin, Lieutenant-Colonel Brancion, and Captains Renvoyé, Vigneron, Grébillet, with their great military caps put on crosswise, these alone felt no anxiety. They would have mur dered and burnt everything for the Emperor. The governor even laughed, and said that he would surrender the city when the shells set his pocket-handkerchief on fire. Judge from this, how much sense such a being had!

While they were reviewing us, groups of the aged and infirm, of women and children, passed across the square on their way to the casemates.

I saw our little wagon go by with the roll of coverings and mattresses on it. The old rabbi was between the shafts—Säfel pushed behind. Sorlé carried David, and Zeffen Esdras. They were walking in the mud, with their hair loose as if they were escaping from a fire; but they did not speak, and went on silently in the midst of that great trouble.

I would have given my life to go and help them —I must stay in the ranks. Ah, the old men of my time have seen terrible things! How often have they thought:—"Happy is he who lives alone in the world; he suffers only for himself, he does not see those whom he loves weeping and groaning, without the power to help them."

Immediately after the review, detachments of citizen gunners were sent to the armories to man the pieces, the firemen were sent to the old market to get out the pumps, and the rest of us, with half a battalion of the Sixth Light Infantry, were sent to the guard-house on the square, to relieve the guards and supply patrols.

The two other battalions had already gone to the advance-posts of Trois-Maisons, of La Fontaine-du-Chateau,—to the block-houses, the half moons, the Ozillo farm, and the Maisons-Rouges, outside of the city.

Our post at the mayoralty consisted of thirty-two men; sixteen soldiers of the line below, commanded by Lieutenant Schmindret, and sixteen of the national guard above, commanded by Desplaces Jacob. We used Burrhus' lodging for our guard-house. It was a large hall with six-inch planks, and beams such as you do not find now-a-days in our forests. A large, round, cast-iron stove, standing on a slab four feet square, was in the left-hand corner, near the door; the zigzag pipes went into the chimney at the right, and piles of wood covered the floor.

It seems as if I were now in that hall. The melted snow which we shook off on entering ran along the floor. I have never seen a sadder day than that; not only because the bombshells and balls might rain upon us at any moment, and set everything on fire, but because of the melting snow, and the mud, and the dampness which reached your very bones, and the orders of the sergeant, who did nothing but call out: "Such and such an one, march! Such an one forward, it is your turn!" etc.

And then the jests and jokes of this mass of tilers, and cobblers, and plasterers, with their patched blouses, shoes run down at the heel, and caps without visors, seated in a circle around the stove, with their rags sticking to their backs, *thouing* you like all the rest of their beggarly race: "Moses, pass along the pitcher! Moses, give me some fire!—Ah, rascals of Jews, when a body risks his life to save property, how proud it makes them! Ah, the villains!" And they winked at each other, and pushed each other's elbows, and made up faces askance. Some of them wanted me to go and get some tobacco for them, and pay for it myself! In fine, all sorts of insults, which a respectable man could endure from the rabble!—Yes, it disgusts me whenever I think of it.

In this guard-house, where we burned whole logs of wood as if they were straw, the steaming old rags which came in soaking wet did not smell very pleasantly. I had to go out every minute to the little platform behind the hall, in order to breathe, and the cold water which the wind blew from the spout sent me in again at once.

Afterward, in thinking it over, it has seemed as if, without these troubles, my heart would have broken at the thought of Sorlé, Zeffen, and the children shut up in a cellar, and that these very annoyances preserved my reason.

This lasted till evening. We did nothing but go in and out, sit down, smoke our pipes, and then begin again to walk the pavement in the rain, or remain on duty for hours together at the entrance of the posterns.

Toward nine o'clock, when all was dark without, and nothing was to be heard but the pacing of the patrols, the shouts of the sentries on the ramparts: "Sentries, attention!" and the steps of our men on their rounds up and down the great wooden stairway of the admiralty, the thought suddenly came to me that the Russians had only tried to frighten us, that it meant nothing; and that there would be no shells that night.

In order to be on good terms with the men, I had asked Monborne's permission to go and get a jug full of brandy, which he at once granted. I took advantage of the opportunity to bite a crust and drink a glass of wine at home. Then I went back, and all the men at the station were very friendly; they passed the jug from one to another, and said that my brandy was very good, and that the sergeant would give me leave to go and fill it as often as I pleased.

"Yes, since it is Moses," replied Monborne, "he may have leave, but nobody else."

We were all on excellent terms with each other and nobody thought of bombardment, when a red flash passed along the high windows of the room. We all turned round, and in a few seconds the shell rumbled on the Bigelberg hill. At the same time a second, then a third flash passed, one after the other, through the large dark room, showing us the houses opposite.

You can never have an idea, Fritz, of those first lights at night! Corporal Winter, an old soldier, who grated tobacco for Tribou, stooped down quietly and lighted his pipe, and said: "Well, the dance is beginning!"

Almost instantly we heard a shell burst at the right in the infantry quarters, another at the left in the Piplinger house on the square, and another quite near us in the Hemmerlé house.

I can't help trembling as I think of it now after thirty years.

All the women were in the casemates, except some old servants who did not want to leave their kitchens; they screamed out: "Help! Fire!"

We were all sure that we were lost; only the old soldiers, crooked on their bench by the stove, with their pipes in their mouths, seemed very calm, as people might who have nothing to lose.

What was worst of all, at the moment when our cannon at the arsenal and powder-house began to answer the Russians', and made every pane of glass in the old building rattle, Sergeant Monborne called out: "Somme, Chevreux, Moses, Dubourg: Forward!"

To send fathers of families roaming about through the mud, in danger, at every step, of being struck by bursting shells, tiles, and whole chimneys falling on their backs, is something against nature; the very mention of it makes me perfectly furious.

Somme and the big inn-keeper Chevreux turned round, full of indignation also; they wanted to exclaim: "It is abominable!"

But that rascal of a Monborne was sergeant, and nobody dared speak a word or even give a side-look; and as Winter, the corporal of the round, had taken down his musket, and made a signal for us to go on, we all took our arms and followed him.

As we went down the stairway, you should have seen the red light, flash after flash, lighting up every nook and corner under the stairs and the worm-eaten rafters; you should have heard our twenty-four pounders thunder; the old rat-hole shook to its foundations, and seemed as if it was all falling to pieces. And under the arch below, towards the place d'Armes, this light shone from the snow banks to the tops of the roofs, showing the glittering pavements, the puddles of water, the chimneys, and dormer-windows, and, at the very end of the street, the cavalry barracks, even the sentry in his box near the large gate:—what a sight!

"It is all over! We are all lost!" I thought.

Two shells passed at this moment over the city: they were the first that I had seen; they moved so slowly that I could follow them through the dark sky; both fell in the trenches, behind the hospital. The charge was too heavy, luckily for us.

I did not speak, nor did the others—we kept our thoughts to ourselves. We heard the calls "Sentries, attention!" answered from one bastion to another all around the place, warning us of the terrible danger we were in.

Corporal Winter, with his old faded blouse, coarse cotton cap, stooping shoulders, musket in shoulder-belt, pipe-end between his teeth, and lantern full of tallow swinging at arm's length, walked before us, calling out: "Look out for the shells! Lie flat! Do you hear?"

I have always thought that veterans of this sort despise citizens, and that he said this to frighten us still more.

A little farther on, at the entrance of the cul-de-sac where Cloutier lived, he halted.

"Come on!" he called, for we marched in file without seeing each other. When we had come up to him he said, "There, now, you men, try to keep together! Our patrol is to prevent fire from breaking out anywhere; as soon as we see a shell pass, Moses will run up and snatch the fuse."

He burst into a laugh as he spoke, so that my anger was roused.

"I have not come here to be laughed at," said I; if you take me for a fool, I will throw down my musket and cartridge-box, and go to the casemates."

He laughed harder than ever. "Moses, respect thy superiors, or beware of the court-martial!" said he.

The others would have laughed too, but the shell-flashes began again; they went down the Rampart street, driving the air before them like gusts of wind; the cannon of the arsenal bastion had just fired. At the same time a shell burst in the street of the Capuchins; Spick's chimney and half his roof fell to the ground with a frightful noise.

"Forward! March!" called Winter.

They had now all become sober. We followed the lantern to the French gate. Behind us, in the street of the Capuchins, a dog howled incessantly. Now and then Winter stopped, and we all listened; nothing was stirring, and nothing was to be heard but the dog and the cries: "Sentries, Attention!" The city was as still as death.

We ought to have gone into the guard-house, for there was nothing to be seen; but the lantern went on toward the gate, swinging above the gutter. That Winter had taken too much brandy!

"We are of no use in this street," said Chevreux; "we can't keep the balls from passing."

But Winter kept calling out: "Are you coming?" And we had to obey.

In front of Genodet's stables, where the old barns of the gendarmery begin, a lane turned to the left toward the hospital. This was full of manure and heaps of dirt—a drain in fact. Well, this rascal of a Winter turned into it, and as we could not see our feet without the lantern, we had to follow him. We went groping, under the roofs of the sheds, along the crazy old walls. It seemed as if we should never get out of this gutter; but at last we came out near the hospital in the midst of the great piles of manure, which were heaped against the grating of the sewer.

It seemed a little lighter, and we saw the roof of the French gate, and the line of fortifications black against the sky; and almost immediately I perceived the figure of a man gliding among the trees at the top of the rampart. It was a soldier stooping so that his hands almost touched the ground. They did not fire on this side; the distant flashes passed over the roofs, and did not lighten the streets below.

I caught Winter's arm, and pointed out to him this man; he instantly hid his lantern under his blouse. The soldier whose back was toward us, stood up, and looked round, apparently listening. This lasted for two or three minutes; then he passed over the rampart at the corner of the bastion, and we heard something scrape the wall of the rampart.

Winter immediately began to run, crying out: "A deserter! To the postern!"

We had heard before this of deserters slipping down into the trenches by means of their bayonets. We all ran. The sentry called out: "Who goes there?"

"The citizen patrol," replied Winter.

He advanced, gave the order, and we went down the postern steps like wild beasts.

Below, at the foot of the large bastions built on the rock, we saw nothing but snow, large black stones, and bushes covered with frost. The deserter needed only to keep still under the bushes; our lantern, which shone only for fifteen or twenty feet, might have wandered about till morning without discovering him: and we should ourselves have supposed that he had escaped. But unfortunately for him, fear urged him on, and we saw him in the distance running to the stairs which lead up to the covered ways. He went like the wind.

"Halt! or I fire!" cried Winter; but he did not stop, and we all ran together on his track, calling out "Halt! Halt!"

Winter had given me the lantern so as to run faster; I followed at a distance, thinking to myself: "Moses, if this man is taken, thou will be the cause of his death." I wanted to put out the lantern, but if Winter had seen me he would have been capable of knocking me down with the butt-end of his musket. He had for a long time been hoping for the cross, and was all the time expecting it and the pension with it.

The deserter ran, as I said, to the stairs. Suddenly he perceived that the ladder, which takes the place of the eight lower steps, was taken away, and he stopped, stupefied! We came nearer—he heard us and began to run faster, to the right toward the half-moon. The poor devil rolled over the snowbanks. Winter aimed at him, and called out: "Halt! Surrender!"

But he got up and began to run again.

Behind the out-works, under the drawbridge, we thought we had lost him: the corporal called to me, "Come along! A thousand thunders!" and at that moment we saw him leaning against the wall, as pale as death. Winter took him by the collar and said: "I have got you!"

Then he tore an epaulette from his shoulder: "You are not worthy to wear that!" said he; "come along!"

He dragged him out of his corner, and held the lantern before his face. We saw a handsome boy of eighteen or nineteen, tall and slender, with small, light moustaches, and blue eyes.

Seeing him there so pale, with Winter's fist at his throat, I thought of the poor boy's father and mother; my heart smote me, and I could not help saying: "Come, Winter, he is a child, a mere child! He will not do it again!"

But Winter, who thought that now surely his cross was won, turned upon me furiously:

"I tell thee what, Jew, stop, or I will run my bayonet through thy body!"

"Wretch!" thought I, "what will not a man do to make sure of his glass of wine for the rest of his days?"

I had a sort of horror of that man; there are wild beasts in the human race!

Chevreux, Somme, and Dubourg did not speak.

Winter began to walk toward the postern, with his hand on the deserter's collar.

"If he stops," said he, "strike him on the back with your muskets! Ah, scoundrel, you desert in the face of the enemy! Your case is clear: next Sunday you will sleep under the turf of the half-moon! Will you come on? Strike him with the butt-end, you cowards!"

What pained me most was to hear the poor fellow's heavy sighs; he breathed so hard, from his fright at being taken, and knowing that he would be shot, that we could hear him fifteen paces off; the sweat ran down my forehead. And now and then he turned to me and gave me such a look as I shall never forget, as if to say: "Save me!"

If I had been alone with Dubourg and Chevreux, we would have let him go; but Winter would sooner have murdered him.

We came in this way to the foot of the postern. They made the deserter pass first. When we reached the top, a sergeant, with four men from the next station, was already there, waiting for us.

"What is it?" asked the sergeant.

"A deserter," said Winter.

The sergeant—an old man—looked at him, and said: "Take him to the station."

"No," said Winter, "he will go with us to the station on the square."

"I will reinforce you with two men," said the sergeant.

"We do not need them," replied Winter roughly. "We took him ourselves, and we are enough to guard him."

The sergeant saw that we ought to have all the glory of it, and he said no more.

We started off again, shouldering our arms; the prisoner, all in tatters and without his shako, walked in the midst.

We soon came to the little square; we had only to cross the old market before reaching the guardhouse. The cannon of the arsenal were firing all the time; as we were starting to leave the market, one of the flashes lighted up the arch in front of us; the prisoner saw the door of the jail at the left, with its great locks, and the sight gave him terrible strength; he tore off his collar, and threw himself from us with both arms stretched out behind.

Winter had been almost thrown down, but he threw himself at once upon the deserter, exclaiming, "Ah, scoundrel, you want to run away!"

We saw no more, for the lantern fell to the ground

"Guard! guard!" cried Chevreux.

All this took but a moment, and half of the infantry post were already there under arms. Then we saw the prisoner again; he was sitting on the edge of the stairway among the pillars; blood was running from his mouth; not more than half his waistcoat was left, and he was bent forward, trembling from head to foot.

Winter held him by the nape of the neck, and said to Lieutenant Schmindret, who was looking on: "A deserter, Lieutenant! He has tried to escape twice, but Winter was on hand."

"That is right," said the lieutenant. "Let them find the jailer."

Two soldiers went away. A number of our comrades of the national guard had come down, but nobody spoke. However hard men may be, when they see a wretch in such a condition, and think, "the day after to-morrow he will be shot!" everybody is silent, and a good many would even release him if they could.

After some minutes Harmantier arrived with his woollen jacket and his bunch of keys.

The lieutenant said to him, "Lock up this man!"

"Come, get up and walk!" he said to the deserter, who rose and followed Harmantier, while everybody crowded round.

The jailer opened the two massive doors of the prison; the prisoner entered without resistance, and then the large locks and bolts fastened him in.

"Every man return to his post!" said the lieutenant to us. And we went up the steps of the mayoralty.

All this had so upset me that I had not thought of my wife and children. But when once above, in the large warm room, full of smoke, with all that set who were laughing and boasting at having taken a poor, unresisting deserter, the thought that I was the cause of this misery filled my soul with anguish; I stretched myself on the camp-bed, and thought of all the trouble that is in the world, of Zeffen, of Säfel, of my children, who might, perhaps, some day be arrested for not liking war. And the words of the Lord came to my mind, which He spake to Samuel, when the people desired a king:

"Hearken unto the voice of the people in all that they say unto thee; for they have not rejected thee, but they have rejected me, that I should not reign over them. Howbeit yet protest solemnly unto them, and show them the manner of the king that shall reign over them. He will take your sons and appoint them for himself; and some shall run before his chariots. He will set them to make his instruments of war. And he will take your daughters to be cooks and bakers. And he will take your fields and your vineyards, and your olive-yards, even the best of them, and give them to his servants. He will take your men-servants, and your maid-servants, and your goodliest young men. He will take the tenth of your sheep; and ye shall be his servants. And ye shall cry out in that day, and the Lord will not hear you."

These thoughts made me very wretched; my only consolation was in knowing that my sons Frômel and Itzig were in America. I resolved to send Säfel, David, and Esdras there also, when the time should come.

These reveries lasted till daylight. I heard no longer the shouts of laughter or the jokes of the ragamuffins. Now and then they would come and shake me, and say, "Go, Moses, and fill your brandy jug! The sergeant gives you leave."

But I did not wish to hear them.

About four o'clock in the morning, our arsenal cannon having dismounted the Russian howitzers on the Quatre-Vents hill, the patrols ceased.

Exactly at seven we were relieved. We went down, one by one, our muskets on our shoulders. We were ranged before the mayoralty, and Captain Vigneron gave the orders: "Carry arms! **Present arms!** Shoulder arms! Break ranks!"

We all dispersed, very glad to get rid of glory.

I was going to run at once to the casemates when I had laid aside my musket, to find Sorlé, Zeffen, and the children; but what was my joy at seeing little Sâfel already at our door! As soon as he saw me turn the corner, he ran to me, exclaiming: "We have all come back! We are waiting for you!"

I stooped to embrace him. At that moment Zeffen opened the window above, and showed me her little Esdras, and Sorlé stood laughing behind them. I went up quickly, blessing the Lord for having delivered us from all our troubles, and exclaiming inwardly: "The Lord is merciful and gracious, slow to anger and plenteous in mercy. Let the glory of the Lord endure forever! Let the Lord rejoice in his works!"

XIV.

BURGUET'S VISIT TO THE DESERTER.

I STILL think it one of the happiest moments of my life, Fritz. Scarcely had I come up the stairs when Zeffen and Sorlé were in my arms; the little ones clung to my shoulders, and I felt their lovely full lips on my cheeks; Sâfel held my hand, and I could not speak a word, but my eyes filled with tears.

Ah! if we had had Baruch with us, how happy we should have been!

At length I went to lay aside my musket, and hang my cartridge-box in the alcove. The children were laughing, and joy was in the house once more. And when I came back in my old beaver cap, and my large, warm woollen stockings, and sat down in the old arm-chair, in front of the little table set with poringers, in which Zeffen was pouring the soup; when I was again in the midst of all these happy faces, bright eyes, and outstretched hands, I could have sung like an old lark on his branch, over the nest where his little ones were opening their beaks and flapping their wings.

I blessed them in my heart a hundred times over. Sorlé, who saw in my eyes what I was thinking, said: "They are all together, Moses, just as they were yesterday; the Lord has preserved them."

"Yes, blessed be the name of the Lord, forever and ever!" I replied.

While we were at breakfast, Zeffen told me about their going to the large casemate at the barracks, how it was full of people stretched on their mattresses in every direction—the cries of some, the fright of others, the torment from the vermin, the water dropping from the arch, the crowds of children who could not sleep, and did nothing but cry, the lamentations of five or six old men who kept calling out, "Ah! our last hour has come! Ah! how cold it is! Ah! we shall never go home—it is all over!"——

Then suddenly the deep silence of all, when they heard the cannon about ten o'clock—the reports, coming slowly at first, then like the roar of a tempest—the flashes, which could be seen even through the blindages of the gate, and old Christine Evig telling her beads as loud as if she were in a procession, and the other women responding together.

As she told me this, Zeffen clasped her little Esdras tightly, while I held David on my knees, embracing him as I thought to myself, "Yes, my poor children, you have been through a great deal!"

Notwithstanding the joy of seeing that we were all safe, the thought of the deserter in his dungeon at the town-house would come to me; he too had parents! And when you think of all the trouble which a father and mother have in bringing up a child, of the nights spent in soothing his cries, of their cares when he is sick, of their hopes in seeing him growing up; and then imagine to yourself some old soldiers sitting around a table to try him, and coolly send him to be shot behind the bastion, it makes you shudder, especially when you say to yourself: "But for me, this boy would have been at liberty; he would be on the road to his village; to-morrow perhaps he would have reached the poor old people's door, and have called out to them, 'Open! it is I!'"

Such thoughts are enough to make one wild.

I did not dare to speak to my wife and children of the poor fellow's arrest; I kept my thoughts to myself.

Without, the detachments from La Roulette, Trois-Maisons, and La Fontaine-du-Château, passed through the street, keeping step; groups of children ran about the city to find the pieces of shells; neigh bors collected to talk about the events of the night —the roofs torn off, chimneys thrown down, the frights they had had. We heard their voices rising and falling, and their shouts of laughter. And I have since seen that it is always the same thing after a bombardment; the shower is forgotten as soon as it is over, and they exclaim: "Huzza! the enemy is routed!"

While we were there meditating, some one came up the stairs. We listened, and our sergeant, with his musket on his shoulder, and his cape and gaiters covered with mud, opened the door, exclaiming: "Good for you, Father Moses! Good for you!— You distinguished yourself last night!"

"Ha! what is it, sergeant?" asked my wife in astonishment.

"What! has he not told you of the famous thing he did, Madame Sorlé? Has he not told you that the national guard Moses, on patrol about nine o'clock at the Hospital bastion, discovered and then arrested a deserter in the very act! It is on Lieutenant Schmindret's affidavit!"

"But I was not alone," I exclaimed in despair; "there were four of us."

"Bah! You discovered the track, you went down into the trenches, you carried the lantern! Father Moses, you must not try to make your good deed seem less; you are wrong. You are going to be named for corporal. The court-martial will sit to-morrow at nine. Be easy, they will take care of your man!"

Imagine, Fritz, how I looked; Sorlé, Zeffen, and the children looked at me, and I did not know what to say.

"Now I must go and change my clothes," said the sergeant, shaking my hand. "We will talk about it again, Father Moses. I always said that you would turn out well in the end."

He gave a low laugh as was his custom, winking his eyes, and then went across the passage into his room.

My wife was very pale.

"Is it true, Moses?" she asked after a minute.

"He! I did not know that he wanted to desert, Sorlé," I replied. "And then the boy ought to have looked round on all sides; he ought to have gone down on the Hospital square, gone round the dunghills, and even into the lane to see if any one was coming; he brought it on himself; I did not know anything, I——"

But Sorlé did not let me finish.

"Run quickly, Moses, to Burguet's!" she exclaimed; "if this man is shot, his blood will be upon our children. Make haste, do not lose a minute."

She raised her hands, and I went out, much troubled.

My only fear was that I should not find Burguet at home; fortunately, on opening his door, on the first floor of the old Canchois house, I saw the tall barber Vésenaire shaving him, in the midst of the old books and papers which filled the room.

Burguet was sitting with the towel at his chin.

"Ah! It is you, Moses!" he exclaimed, in a glad tone. "What gives me the pleasure of a visit from you?"

"I come to ask a favor of you, Burguet."

"If it is for money," said he, "we shall have difficulty."

He laughed, and his servant-woman Marie Loriot, who heard us from the kitchen, opened the door, and thrust her red head-gear into the room, as she called out, "I think that we shall have difficulty! We owe Vésenaire for three months' shaving; do not we, Vésenaire?"

She said this very seriously, and Burguet, instead of being angry, began to laugh. I have always fancied that a man of his talents had a sort of need of such an incarnation of human stupidity to laugh at, and help his digestion. He never was willing to dismiss this Marie Loriot.

In short, while Vésenaire kept on shaving him, I

gave him an account of our patrol and the arrest of the deserter; and begged him to defend the poor fellow. I told him that he alone was able to save him, and restore peace, not only to my own mind, but to Sorlé, Zeffen, and the whole family, for we were all in great distress, and we depended entirely upon him to help us.

"Ah! you take me at my weak point, Moses! If it is possible for me to save this man, I must try. But it will not be an easy matter. During the last fortnight, desertions have begun—the court-martial wishes to make an example. It is a bad business. You have money, Moses; give Vésenaire four sous to go and take a drop."

I gave four sous to Vésenaire, who made a grand bow and went out. Burguet finished dressing himself.

"Let us go and see!" said he, taking me by the arm.

And we went down together on our way to the mayoralty.

Many years have passed since that day. Ah, well! it seems now as if we were going under the arch, and I heard Burguet saying: "Hey, sergeant! Tell the turnkey that the prisoner's advocate is here."

Harmantier came, bowed, and opened the door

We went down into the dungeon full of stench, and saw in the right-hand corner a figure gathered in a heap on the straw.

"Get up!" said Harmantier, "here is your advocate."

The poor wretch moved and raised himself in the darkness. Burguet leaned toward him and said: "Come! Take courage! I have come to talk with you about your defence."

And the other began to sob.

When a man has been knocked down, torn to tatters, beaten till he cannot stand, when he knows that the law is against him, that he must die without seeing those whom he loves, he becomes as weak as a baby. Those who maltreat their prisoners are great villains.

"Let us see!" said Burguet. "Sit down on the side of your camp-bed. What is your name? Where did you come from? Harmantier, give this man a little water to drink and wash himself!"

"He has some, M. Burguet; he has some in the corner."

"Ah, well!"

"Compose yourself, my boy!"

The more gently he spoke, the more did the poor fellow weep. At last, however, he said that his family lived near Gérarmer, in the Vosges; that his father's name was Mathieu Belin, and that he was a fisherman at Retournemer.

Burguet drew every word out of his mouth; he wanted to know every particular about his father and mother, his brothers and sisters.

I remember that his father had served under the Republic, and had even been wounded at Fleurus; that his oldest brother had died in Russia; that he himself was the second son taken from home by the conscription, and that there were still at home three sisters younger than himself.

This came from him slowly; he was so prostrated by Winter's blows, that he moved and sank down like a soulless body.

There was still another thing, Fritz, as you may think—the boy was young! and that brought to my mind the days when I used to go in two hours from Phalsburg to Marmoutier, to see Sorlé—Ah, poor wretch! As he told all this, sobbing, with his face in his hands, my heart melted within me.

Burguet was quite overcome. When we were leaving, at the end of an hour, he said, "Come, let us be hopeful! You will be tried to-morrow.—Don't despair! Harmantier, we must give this man a cloak; it is dreadfully cold, especially at night. It is a bad business, my boy, but it is not hopeless. Try to appear as well as you can before the audi ence; the court-martial always thinks better of a man who is well-dressed."

When we were out, he said to me: "Moses, you send the man a clean shirt. His waistcoat is torn; don't forget to have him decently dressed every way; soldiers always judge of a man by his appearance."

"Be easy about that," said I.

The prison doors were closed, and we went across the market.

"Now," said Burguet, "I must go in. I must think it over. It is well that the brother was left in Russia, and that the father has been in the service—it is something to make a point of."

We had reached the corner of the Rampart street; he kept on, and I went home more miserable than before.

You cannot imagine, Fritz, how troubled I was; when a man has always had a quiet conscience it is terrible to reproach one's self, and think: "If this man is shot, if his father, and mother, and sisters, and that other one, who is expecting him, are made miserable, thou, Moses, wilt be the cause of it all!"

Fortunately there was no lack of work to be done at home; Sorlé had just opened the old shop to begin to sell our brandies, and it was full of people. For a week the keepers of coffee-houses and inns had had nothing wherewith to fill their casks; they were on the point of shutting up shop. Imagine the crowd! They came in a row, with their jugs and little casks and pitchers. The old topers came too, sticking out their elbows; Sorlé, Zeffen, and Sâfel had not time to serve them.

The sergeant said that we must put a policeman at our door to prevent quarrels, for some of them said that they lost their turn, and that their money was as good as anybody's.

It will be a good many years before such a crowd will be seen again in front of a Phalsburg shop.

I had only time to tell my wife that Burguet would defend the deserter, and then went down into the cellar to fill the two tuns at the counter, which were already empty.

A fortnight after, Sorlé doubled the price; our first two pipes were sold, and this extra price did not lessen the demand.

Men always find money for brandy and tobacco, even when they have none left for bread. This is why governments impose their heaviest taxes upon these two articles; they might be heavier still without diminishing their use—only, children would starve to death.

I have seen this—I have seen this great folly in men, and I am astonished whenever I think of it.

That day we kept on selling until seven o'clock in the evening, when the tattoo was sounded.

My pleasure in making money had made me forget the deserter; I did not think of him again till after supper, when night set in; but I did not say a word about him; we were all so tired and so delighted with the day's profits that we did not want to be troubled with thinking of such things. But after Zeffen and the children had retired, I told Sorlé of our visit to the prisoner. I told her, too, that Burguet had hopes, which made her very happy.

About nine o'clock, by God's blessing, we were all asleep.

XV.

TRIAL OF THE DESERTER.

You can believe, Fritz, that I did not sleep much that night, notwithstanding my fatigue. The thought of the deserter tormented me. I knew that if he should be shot, Zeffen and Sorlé would be inconsolable; and I knew, too, that after three or four years the vile race would say: "Look at this Moses, with his large brown cloak, his cape turned down over the back of his neck, and his respectable look—well, during the blockade he caused the arrest of a poor deserter, who was shot: so much you can trust a Jew's appearance!"

They would have said this, undoubtedly; for the only consolation of villains is to make people think that everybody is like themselves.

And then how often should I reproach myself for this man's death, in times of misfortune or in my old age, when I should not have a minute's peace! How often should I have said that it was a judgment of the Lord, that it was on account of this deserter.

So I wanted to do immediately all that I could, and by six o'clock in the morning I was in my old shop in the market with my lantern, selecting epaulettes and my best clothes. I put them in a napkin and took them to Harmantier at daybreak.

The special council of war, which was called—I do not know why—the *Ventose* council, was to meet at nine o'clock. It was composed of a major, president, four captains, and two lieutenants. Monbrun, the captain of the foreign legion, was judge-advocate, and Brigadier Duphot recorder.

It was astonishing how the whole city knew about it beforehand, and that by seven o'clock the Nicaises, and Pigots, and Vinatiers, etc., had left their rickety quarters, and had already filled the whole mayoralty, the arch, the stairway, and the large room above, laughing, whistling, stamping, as if it were a bear-fight at Klein's inn, the "Ox."

You do not see things like that now-a-days, thank God! men have become more gentle and humane. But after all these wars, a deserter met with less pity than a fox caught in a trap, or a wolf led by the muzzle.

As I saw all this, my courage failed; all my admiration for Burguet's talents could not keep me from thinking:

The man is lost! Who can save him, when this

crowd has come on purpose to see him condemned to death, and led to the Glacière bastion?

I was overwhelmed by the thought.

I went trembling into Harmantier's little room, and said to him: "This is for the deserter; take it to him from me." "All right!" said he.

I asked him if he had confidence in Burguet. He shrugged his shoulders, and said: "We must have examples."

The stamping outside continued, and when I went out there was a great whistling in the balcony, the arch, and everywhere, and shouts of "Moses! hey, Moses! this way!"

But I did not turn my head, and went home very sad.

Sorlé handed me a summons to appear as a witness before the court-martial, which a gendarme had just brought; and till nine o'clock I sat meditating behind the stove, trying to think of some way of escape for the prisoner.

Sâfel was playing with the children; Zeffen and Sorlé had gone down to continue our sales.

A few minutes before nine I started for the town-house, which was already so crowded that, had it not been for the guard at the door, and the gendarmes scattered within the building, the witnesses could hardly have got in.

Just as I got there, Captain Monbrun was beginning to read his report. Burguet sat opposite, with his head leaning on his hand.

They showed me into a little room, where were Winter, Chevreux, Dubourg, and the gendarme Fiegel; so that we didn't hear anything before being called.

On the wall at the right it was written in large letters that any witness who did not tell the truth, should be delivered to the council, and suffer the same penalty as the accused. This made one consider, and I resolved at once to conceal nothing, as was right and sensible. The gendarme also informed us that we were forbidden to speak to each other.

After a quarter of an hour Winter was summoned, and then, at intervals of ten minutes, Chevreux, Dubourg, and myself.

When I went into the court-room, the judges were all in their places; the major had laid his hat on the desk before him; the recorder was mending his pen. Burguet looked at me calmly. Without they were stamping, and the major said to the brigadier:

"Inform the public that if this noise continues, I shall have the mayoralty cleared."

The brigadier went out at once, and the major said to me:

"National guard Moses, make your deposition. What do you know?"

I told it all simply. The deserter at the left, between two gendarmes, seemed more dead than alive. I would gladly have acquitted him of everything; but when a man fears for himself, when old officers in full dress are scowling at you as if they could see through you, the simplest and best way is not to lie. A father's first thought should be for his children! In short, I told everything that I had seen, nothing more or less, and at last the major said to me:

"That is enough; you may go."

But seeing that the others, Winter, Chevreux, Dubourg, remained sitting on a bench at the left, I did the same.

Almost immediately five or six good-for-nothings began to stamp and murmur, "Shoot him! shoot him!" The president ordered the brigadier to arrest them, and in spite of their resistance they were all led to prison. Silence was then established in the court-room, but the stampings without continued.

"Judge-advocate, it is your turn to speak," said the major.

This judge-advocate, who seems now before my eyes, and whom I can almost hear speak, was a man of fifty, short and thick, with a short neck, long, thick, straight nose, very wide forehead, shining black hair, thin moustaches, and bright eyes. While he was listening, his head turned right and left as if on a pivot; you could see his long nose and the corner of his eye, but his elbows did not stir from the table. He looked like one of those large crows which seem to be sleeping in the fields at the close of autumn, and yet see everything that is going on around them.

Now and then he raised his arm as if to draw back his sleeve, as advocates have a way of doing. He was in full dress, and spoke terribly well, in a clear and strong voice, stopping and looking at the people to see if they agreed with him; and if he saw even a slight grimace, he began again at once in some other way, and, as it were, obliged you to understand in spite of yourself.

As he went on very slowly, without hurrying or forgetting anything, to show that the deserter was on the road when we arrested him, that he not only had the intention of escaping, but was already outside of the city, quite as guilty as if he had been found in the ranks of the enemy—as he clearly showed all this, I was angry because he was right, and I thought to myself, "Now, what was there to be said in reply."

And then, when he said that the greatest of crimes was to abandon one's flag, because one betrays at once his country, his family, all that has a right to his life, and makes himself unworthy to live; when he said that the court would follow the conscience of all who had a heart, of all who held to the honor of France; that he would give a new example of his zeal for the safety of the country and the glory of the emperor; that he would show the new recruits that they could only succeed by doing their duty and by obeying orders; when he said all this with terrible power and clearness, and I heard from time to time, a murmur of assent and admiration, then, Fritz, I thought that the Lord alone was able to save that man!

The deserter sat motionless, his arms folded on the dock, and his face upon them. He felt, doubtless, as I did, and every one in the room, and the court itself. Those old men seemed pleased as they heard the judge-advocate express so well what had all along been their own opinion. Their faces showed their satisfaction.

This lasted for more than an hour. The captain sometimes stopped a moment to give his audience time to reflect on what he had said. I have always thought that he must have been attorney-general, or something more dangerous still to deserters.

I remember that he said, in closing, "You will make an example! You will be of one mind. You will not forget that, at this time, firmness in the court is more necessary than ever to the safety of the country."

When he sat down, such a murmur of approbation arose in the room that it reached the stairway at once, and we heard the shouts outside, "*Vive l'Empereur!*"

The major and the other members of the council looked smilingly at each other, as if to say, "It is all settled. What remains is a mere formality!"

The shouts without increased. This lasted more than ten minutes. At last the major said:

"Brigadier, if the tumult continues, clear the town-house! Begin with the court-room!"

There was silence at once, for every one was curious to know what Burguet would say in reply. I would not have given two farthings for the life of the deserter.

"Counsel for the prisoner, you have the floor!" said the major, and Burguet rose.

Now, Fritz, if I had an idea that I could repeat to you what Burguet said, for a whole hour, to save the life of a poor conscript; if I should try to depict his face, the sweetness of his voice, and then his heart-rending cries, and then his silent pauses and his appeals—if I had such an idea, I should consider myself a being full of pride and vanity!

No; nothing finer was ever heard. It was not a man speaking; it was a mother, trying to snatch her babe from death! Ah! what a great thing it is to have this power of moving to tears those who hear us! But we ought not to call it talent, it is heart.

"Who is there without faults? Who does not need pity?"

This is what he said, as he asked the council if they could find a perfectly blameless man; if evil thoughts never came to the bravest; if they had never, for even a day or a moment, had the thought of running away to their native village, when they were young, when they were eighteen, when father and mother and the friends of their childhood were living, and they had not another in the world. A poor child without instruction, without knowledge of the world, brought up at hap-hazard, thrown into the army—what could you expect of him? What fault of his could not be pardoned? What does he know of country, the honor of his flag, the glory of his majesty? Is it not later in life that these great ideas come to him?

And then he asked those old men if they had not a son, if they were sure that, even at that moment, that son were not committing an offence which was liable to the punishment of death. He said to them:

"Plead for him! What would you say? You would say, 'I am an old soldier. For thirty years I have shed my blood for France. I have grown gray upon the battle-fields, I am riddled with wounds, I have gained every rank at the point of the sword. Ah, well! take my epaulettes, take my decorations, take everything; but save my child! Let my blood be the ransom for his offence! He does not know the greatness of his crime; he is too young; he is a conscript; he loved us; he longed to embrace us, and then go back again—he loved a maiden. Ah! you, too, have been young! Pardon him. Do not disgrace an old soldier in his son.'

"Perhaps you could say, too, 'I had other sons. They died for their country. Let their blood answer for his, and give me back this one—the last that I have left!'

"This is what you would say, and far better than I, because you would be the father, the old soldier speaking of his own services! Well, the father of this youth could speak like you! He is an old soldier of the Republic! He went with you, perhaps, when the Prussians entered Champagne! He was wounded at Fleurus! He is an old comrade in arms! His oldest son was left behind in Russia!"

And Burguet turned pale as he spoke. It seemed as if grief had robbed him of his strength, and he were about to fall. The silence was so great that we heard the breathing throughout the court-room. The deserter sobbed. Everybody thought, "It is done! Burguet need say no more! It must be that he has gained his cause!"

But all at once he began again in another and more tender manner. Speaking slowly, he described the life of a poor peasant and his wife, who had but one comfort, one solitary hope on earth—their child! As we listened we saw these poor people, we heard them talk together, we saw over the door the old chapeau of the time of the Republic. And when we were thinking only of this, suddenly Burguet showed us the old man and his wife learning that their son had been killed, not by Russians or Germans, but by Frenchmen. We heard the old man's cry!

But it was terrible, Fritz! I wanted to run away. The officers of the council, several of whom were married men, looked before them with fixed eyes, and clenched hands; their gray moustaches shook. The major had raised his hand two or three times, as if to signify that it was enough, but Burguet had always something still more powerful, more just, more grand to add. His plea lasted till nearly eleven, when he sat down. There was not a murmur to be heard in the three rooms nor outside. And the Judge-advocate on the other side began again, saying that all that signified nothing, that it was unfortunate for the father that his son was unworthy, that every man clung to his children, that soldiers must be taught not to desert in face of the enemy; that, if the court yielded to such arguments, nobody would ever be shot, discipline would be utterly destroyed, the army could not exist, and that the army was the strength and glory of the country.

Burguet replied almost immediately. I cannot recall what he said; my head could not hold so many things at once: but I shall never forget this, that about one o'clock, the council having sent us away that they might deliberate — the prisoner meanwhile having been taken back to his cell — after a few minutes we were allowed to return, and the major, standing on the platform where conscriptions were drawn, declared that the accused Jean Balin was acquitted, and gave the order for his immediate release.

It was the first acquittal since the departure of the Spanish prisoners before the blockade; the rowdies, who had come in crowds to see a man condemned and shot, could not believe it; several of them exclaimed: "We are cheated!"

But the major ordered Brigadier Descarmes to take the names of these brawlers, so that they should be seen to; then the whole mass trampled down the stairs in five minutes, and we, in our turn, were able to descend.

I had taken Burguet by the arm, my eyes full of tears.

"Are you satisfied, Moses?" said he, already quite his own joyous self again.

"Burguet!" said I, "Aaron himself, the own brother of Moses, and the greatest orator of Israel, could not have spoken better than you did; it was admirable! I owe my peace of mind to you! Whatever you may ask for so great a service I am ready to give to the extent of my means."

We went down the stairs; the members of the council following us thoughtfully, one by one. Burguet smiled.

"Do you mean it, Moses?" said he, stopping under the arch.

"Yes, here is my hand."

"Very well!" said he, "I ask you to give me a good dinner at the *Ville-de-Metz.*"

"With all my heart!"

Several citizens, Father Parmentier, Cochois the

tax-gatherer, and Adjutant Muller, were waiting for Burguet at the foot of the mayoralty steps, to congratulate him. As they were surrounding and shaking hands with him, Säfel came and rushed into my arms; Zeffen had sent him to learn the news. I embraced him, and said joyously: "Go, tell your mother that we have won! Take your dinner. I am going to dine at the *Ville-de-Metz* with Burguet. Make haste, my child!"

He started running.

"You dine with me, Burguet," said Father Parmentier.

"Thank you, Mr. Mayor, I am engaged to dine with Moses; I will go at another time."

And, with our arms around each other, we entered Mother Barrière's large corridor, where there was still the odor of good roasts, in spite of the blockade.

"Listen, Burguet," said I; "we are going to dine alone, and you shall choose whatever wines and dishes you like best; you know them better than I do."

I saw his eyes sparkle.

"Good! good!" said he, "it is understood."

In the large dining-hall the war-commissioner and two officers were dining together; they turned round, and we saluted them.

I sent for Mother Barrère, who came at once, her

apron on her arm, as smiling and chubby as usual. Burguet whispered a couple of words in her ear, and she instantly opened the door at the right, and said:

"Walk in, gentlemen, walk in! You will not have to wait long."

We went into the square room at the corner of the square, a small, high room, with two large windows covered with muslin curtains, and the porcelain stove well heated, as it should be in winter.

A servant came to lay the table, while we warmed our hands upon the marble.

"I have a good appetite, Moses; my pleading is going to cost you dear," said Burguet, laughing.

"So much the better; it cannot be too dear for the gratitude I owe you."

"Come," said he, putting his hand on my shoulder, "I won't ruin you, but we must have a good dinner."

When the table was ready, we sat down, opposite each other, in soft, comfortable arm-chairs; and Burguet, fastening his napkin in his button-hole, as was his custom, took up the bill of fare. He pondered over it a long time; for you know, Fritz, that though nightingales are good singers, they have the sharpest beaks in the world. Burguet was like them, and I was delighted at seeing him thus meditating.

At last he said to the servant, slowly and solemnly:

"This and that, Madeleine, cooked so and so. And such a wine to begin with, and such another at the end."

"Very well, M. Burguet," replied Madeleine, as she went out.

Two minutes afterward she brought us a good toast soup. During a blockade this was something greatly to be desired; three weeks later we should have been very fortunate to have got one.

Then she brought us some Bordeaux wine, warmed in a napkin. But you do not suppose, Fritz, that I am going to tell you all the details of this dinner? although I remember it all, with great pleasure, to this day. Believe me, there was nothing wanting, meats nor fresh vegetables, nor the large well-smoked ham, nor any of the things which are dreadfully scarce in a shut-up city. We had even salad! Madame Barrière had kept it in the cellar, in earth, and Burguet wished to dress it himself with olive oil. We had, too, the last juicy pears which were seen in Phalsburg, during that winter of 1814.

Burguet seemed happy, especially when the bottle

of old Lircncourt was brought, and we drank together.

"Moses," said he with softened eyes, "if all my pleas had as good pay as you give, I would resign my place in college; but this is the first fee I have received."

"And if I were in your place, Burguet," I exclaimed, "instead of staying in Phalsburg, I would go to a large city. You would have plenty of good dinners, good hotels, and the rest would soon follow."

"Ah! twenty years ago this might have been good advice," said he, rising, "but it is too late now. Let us go and take our coffee, Moses."

Thus it is that men of great talents often bury themselves in small places, where nobody values them at their true worth; they fall gradually into their own ruts, and disappear without notice.

Burguet never forgot to go to the coffee-house at about five o'clock, to play a game of cards with the old Jew Solomon, whose trade it was. Burguet and five or six citizens fully supported this man, who took his beer and coffee twice a day at their expense, to say nothing of the crowns he pocketed for the support of his family.

So far as the others were concerned, I was not surprised at this, for they were fools! but for a man like Burguet I was always astonished at it; for, out of twenty deals, Solomon did not let them win more than one or two, with the risk before his eyes of losing his best practice, by discouraging them altogether.

I had explained this fifty times to Burguet; he assented, and kept on all the same.

When we reached the coffee-house, Solomon was already there, in the corner of a window at the left —his little dirty cap on his nose, and his old greasy frock hanging at the foot of the stool. He was shuffling the cards all by himself. He looked at Burguet out of the corner of his eye, as a birdcatcher looks at larks, as if to say:

"Come! I am here! I am expecting you!"

But Burguet, when with me, dared not obey the old man; he was ashamed of his weakness, and merely made a little motion of his head while he seated himself at the opposite table, where coffee was served to us.

The comrades came soon, and Solomon began to fleece them. Burguet turned his back to them; I tried to divert his attention, but his heart was with them; he listened to all the throws, and yawned in his hand.

About seven o'clock, when the room was full of smoke, and the balls were rolling on the billiard tables, suddenly a young man, a soldier, entered, looking round in all directions.

It was the deserter.

He saw us at last, and approached us with his foraging cap in his hand. Burguet looked up and recognized him; I saw him turn red; the deserter, on the contrary, was very pale; he tried to speak, but could not say a word.

"Ah! my friend!" said Burguet, "here you are, safe!"

"Yes, sir," replied the conscript, "and I have come to thank you for myself, for my father, and for my mother!"

"Ah!" said Burguet, coughing, "it is all right! it is all right!"

He looked tenderly at the young man, and asked him softly, "You are glad to live?"

"Oh! yes, sir," replied the conscript, "very glad."

"Yes," said Burguet, in a low voice, looking at the clock; "it would have been all over now! Poor child!"

And suddenly beginning to use the *thou* he said, "Thou hast had nothing with which to drink my health, and I have not another sou. Moses, give him a hundred sous."

I gave him ten francs. The deserter tried to thank me.

"That is good!" said Burguet, rising. "Go and take a drink with thy comrades. Be happy, and do not desert again."

He made as if he would follow Solomon's playing; but when the deserter said, "I thank you, too, for her who is expecting me!" he looked at me sideways, not knowing what to answer, so much was he moved. Then I said to the conscript, "We are very glad that we have been of assistance to you; go and drink the health of your advocate, and behave yourself well."

He looked at us for a moment longer, as if he were unable to move; we saw his thanks in his face, a thousand times better than he had been able to utter them. At length he slowly went out, saluting us, and Burguet finished his cup of coffee.

We meditated for some minutes upon what had passed. But soon the thought of seeing my family seized me.

Burguet was like a soul in purgatory. Every minute he got up to look on, as one or another played, with his hands crossed behind his back; then he sat down with a melancholy look. I should have been very sorry to plague him longer, and, as the clock struck eight, I bade him good-evening, which evidently pleased him.

"Good-night, Moses," said he, leading me to the

door. "My compliments to Madame Sorlé, and Madame Zeffen."

"Thank you! I shall not forget it."

I went, very glad to return home, where I arrived in a few minutes. Sorlé saw at once that I was in good spirits, for, meeting her at the door of our little kitchen, I embraced her joyfully.

"It is all right, Sorlé," said I, "all just right!"

"Yes," said she, "I see that it is all right!"

She laughed, and we went into the room where Zeffen was undressing David. The poor little fellow, in his shirt, came and offered me his cheek to kiss. Whenever I dined in the city, I used to bring him some of the dessert, and, in spite of his sleepy eyes, he soon found his way to my pockets.

You see, Fritz, what makes grandfathers happy is to find out how bright and sensible their grandchildren are.

Even little Esdras, whom Sorlé was rocking, understood at once that something unusual was going on; he stretched out his little hands to me, as if to say, "I like cake too!"

We were all of us very happy. At length, having sat down, I gave them an account of the day, setting forth the eloquence of Burguet, and the poor deserter's happiness. They all listened attentively.

Sâfel, seated on my knees, whispered to me, "We have sold three hundred francs' worth of brandy!"

This news pleased me greatly: when one makes an outlay, he ought to profit by it.

About ten o'clock, after Zeffen had wished us good-night, I went down and shut the door, and put the key underneath for the sergeant, if he should come in late.

While we were going to bed, Sorlé repeated what Sâfel had said, adding that we should be in easy circumstances when the blockade was over, and that the Lord had helped us in the midst of great calamities.

We were happy and without fear of the future.

XVI.

A SORTIE OF THE GARRISON.

Nothing extraordinary occurred for several days. The governor had the plants and bushes growing in the crevices of the ramparts torn away, to make desertion less easy, and he forbade the officers being too rough with the men, which had a good effect.

At this time, hundreds of thousands of Austrians, Russians, Bavarians, and Wurtemburgers, by squadrons and regiments, passed around the city beyond range of our cannon, and marched upon Paris.

Then there were terrible battles in Champagne, but we knew nothing of them.

The uniforms changed every day outside the city; our old soldiers on top of the ramparts recognized all the different nations they had been fighting for twenty years.

Our sergeant came regularly after the call, to take me upon the arsenal bastion; citizens were there all the time, talking about the invasion, which did not, come to an end.

It was wonderful! In the direction of St. Jean, on the edge of the forest of La Bonne Fontaine, we saw, for hours at a time, cavalry and infantry defiling, and then convoys of powder and balls, and then cannon, and then files of bayonets, helmets, red, and green, and blue coats, lances, peasants' wagons covered with cloth—all these passed, passed like a river.

On this broad white plateau, surrounded by forests, we could see everything.

Now and then some Cossacks or dragoons would leave the main body, and push on galloping to the very foot of the glacis, in the lane *des Dames*, or near the little chapel. Instantly one of our old marine artillerymen would stretch out his gray moustaches upon a rampart gun, and slowly take aim; the bystanders would all gather round him, even the children, who would creep between your legs, fearless of balls or shells—and the heavy riflegun would go off!

Many a time I have seen the Cossack or Uhlan fall from his saddle, and the horse rush back to the squadron with his bridle on his neck. The people would shout with joy; they would climb up on the ramparts and look down, and the gunner would rub his hands and say, "One more out of the way!"

At other times these old men, with their ragged cloaks full of holes, would bet a couple of sous as to who should bring down this sentinel or that vidette, on the Mittelbronn or Bigelberg hill.

It was so far that they needed good eyes to see the one they designated; but these men, accustomed to the sea, can discern everything as far as the eye can reach.

"Come, Paradis, there he is!" one would say.

"Yes, there he is! Lay down your two sous; there are mine!"

And they would fire. They would go on as if it were a game of ninepins. God knows how many men they killed for the sake of their two sous. Every morning about nine o'clock I found these marines in my shop, drinking "to the Cossack," as they said. The last drop they poured into their hands, to strengthen their nerves, and started off with rounded backs, calling out:

"Hey! good-day, Father Moses! The kaiserlick is vey well!"

I do not think that I ever saw so many people in my life as in those months of January and February, 1814; they were like the locusts of Egypt! How the earth could produce so many people I could not comprehend.

I was naturally greatly troubled on account of it, and the other citizens also, as I need not say; but our sergeant laughed and winked.

"Look, Father Moses!" said he, pointing from Quatre-Vents to Bigelberg—"all these that are passing by, all that have passed, and all that are going to pass, are to enrich the soil of Champagne and Lorraine! The Emperor is down there, waiting for them in a good place—he will fall upon them! The thunderbolt of Austerlitz, of Jena, of Wagram, is all ready—it can wait no longer! Then they will file back in retreat; but our armies will follow them, with our bayonets in their backs, and we shall go out from here, and flank them off. Not one shall escape. Their account is settled. And then will be the time for you to have old clothes and other things to sell, Father Moses! He! he! he! How fat you will grow!"

He was merry at the thought of it; but you may suppose, Fritz, that I did not count much upon those uniforms that were running across the fields; I would much rather they had been a thousand leagues away.

Such are men—some are glad and others miserable from the same cause. The sergeant was so confident that sometimes he persuaded me, and I thought as he did.

We would go down the Rampart street together; he would go to the cantine where they had begun to distribute siege-rations, or perhaps he would go home with me, take his little glass of cherry-brandy, and explain to me the Emperor's grand strokes since '96 in Italy. I did not understand anything about it, but I made believe that I understood, which answered all the purpose.

There came envoys, too, sometimes on the road from Nancy, sometimes from Saverne or Metz. They raised, at a distance, the little white flag; one of their trumpeters sounded and then withdrew; the officer of the guard received the envoy and bandaged his eyes, then he went under escort through the city to the governor's house. But what these envoys told or demanded never transpired in the city; the council of defence alone were informed of it.

We lived confined within our walls as if we were in the middle of the sea, and you cannot believe how that weighs upon one after a while, how depressing and overpowering it is not to be able to go out even upon the glacis. Old men who had been nailed for ten years to their arm-chairs, and who never thought of moving, were oppressed by grief at knowing that the gates remained shut. And then every one wants to know what is going on, to see strangers and talk of the affairs of the country—no one knows how necessary these things are until he has had experience like ours. The meanest peasant, the lowest man in Dagsburg who might have chanced to come into the city, would have been received like a god; everybody would have run to see him and ask for the news from France.

Ah! those are right who hold that liberty is the greatest of blessings, for it is insupportable being shut up in a prison—let it be as large as France. Men are made to come and go, to talk and write, and live together, to carry on trade, to tell the news; and if you take these from them, you leave nothing desirable.

Governments do not understand this simple matter; they think that they are stronger when they prevent men from living at their ease, and at last everybody is tired of them. The true power of a sovereign is always in proportion to the liberty he can give, and not to that which he is obliged to take away. The allies had learned this for Napoleon, and thence came their confidence.

The saddest thing of all was that, toward the end of January, the citizens began to be in want. I cannot say that money was scarce, because a centime never went out of the city; but everything was dear;

what three weeks before was worth two sous now cost twenty! This has often led me to think that scarcity of money is one of the fooleries invented by scoundrels to deceive the weak-minded. What else can make money scarce? You are not poor with two sous, if they are enough to buy your bread, wine, meat, clothes, etc.; but if you need twenty times more to buy these things, then not only are you poor, but the whole country is poor. There is no want of money when everything is cheap; it is always scarce when the necessaries of life are dear.

So, when people are shut up as we were, it is very fortunate to be able to sell more than you buy. My brandy sold for three francs the quart, but at the same time we needed bread, oil, potatoes, and their prices were all proportionately high.

One morning old Mother Quéru came to my shop weeping; she had eaten nothing for two days! and yet that was the least thing, said she; she missed nothing but her glass of wine, which I gave her gratis. She gave me a hundred blessings and went away happy. A good many others would have liked their glass of wine! I have seen old men in despair because they had nothing to snuff; they even went so far as to snuff ashes; some at this time smoked the leaves of the large walnut-tree by the arsenal, and liked it well.

Unfortunately, all this was but the beginning of

want: later we learned to fast for the glory of his majesty.

Toward the end of February, it became cold again. Every evening they fired a hundred shells upon us, but we became accustomed to all that, till it seemed quite a thing of course. As soon as the shell burst everybody ran to put out the fire, which was an easy matter, since there were tubs full of water ready in every house.

Our guns replied to the enemy; but as after ten o'clock the Russians fired only with field-pieces, our men could aim only at their fire, which was changing continually, and it was not easy to reach them.

Sometimes the enemy fired incendiary balls; these are balls pierced with three nails in a triangle, and filled with such inflammable matter that it could be extinguished only by throwing the ball under water, which was done.

We had as yet had no fires; but our outposts had fallen back, and the allies drew closer and closer around the city. They occupied the Ozillo farm, Pernette's tile-kiln, and the Maisons-Rouges, which had been abandoned by our troops. Here they intended to pass the winter pleasantly. These were Wurtemburg, Bavarian, and Baden troops, and other landwehr, who replaced in Alsace the regular troops that had left for the interior.

We could plainly see their sentinels in long, grayish blue coats, flat helmets, and muskets on their shoulders, walking slowly in the poplar alley which leads to the tile-kiln.

From thence these troops could any moment, on a dark night, enter the trenches, and even attempt to force a postern.

They were in large numbers and denied themselves nothing, having three or four villages around them to furnish their provisions, and the great fires of the tile-kiln to keep them warm.

Sometimes a Russian battalion relieved them, but only for a day or two, being obliged to continue its route. These Russians bathed in the little pond behind the building, in spite of the ice and snow which filled it.

All of them, Russians, Wurtemburgers, and Baden men, fired upon our sentinels, and we wondered that our governor had not stopped them with our balls. But one day the sergeant came in joyfully, and whispered to me, winking:

"Get up early to-morrow morning, Father Moses; don't say a word to any one, and follow me. You will see something that will make you laugh."

"All right, sergeant!" said I.

He went to bed at once, and long before day, about five o'clock, I heard him jump out of bed, which astonished me the more, as I had not heard the call.

I rose softly. Sorlé sleepily asked me: "What is it, Moses?"

"Go to sleep again, Sorlé," I replied; "the sergeant told me that he wanted to show me something."

She said no more, and I finished dressing myself.

Just then the sergeant knocked at the door; I blew out the candle, and we went down. It was very dark.

We heard a faint noise in the direction of the barracks; the sergeant went toward it, saying: "Go up on the bastion; we are going to attack the tile-kiln."

I ran up the street at once. As I came upon the ramparts I saw in the shadow of the bastion on the right our gunners at their pieces. They did not stir, and all around was still; matches lighted and set in the ground gave the only light, and shone like stars in the darkness.

Five or six citizens, in the secret, like myself, stood motionless at the entrance of the postern. The usual cries, "Sentries, Attention!" were answered around the city; and without, from the part of the enemy, we heard the cries "*Verdà!*" and "*Souïda!*"*

---

* Who goes there?

It was very cold, a dry cold, notwithstanding the fog.

Soon, from the direction of the square in the interior of the city, a number of men went up the street; if they had kept step the enemy would have heard them from the distance upon the glacis; but they came pell-mell, and turned near us into the postern stair-way. It took full ten minutes for them to pass. You can imagine whether I watched them, and yet I could not recognize our sergeant in the darkness.

The two companies formed again in the trenches after their defiling, and all was still.

My feet were perfectly numb, it was so cold; but curiosity kept me there.

At last, after about half an hour, a pale line stretched behind the bottom-land of Fiquet, around the woods of La Bonne Fontaine. Captain Rolfo, the other citizens, and myself, leaned against the rampart, and looked at the snow-covered plain, where some German patrols were wandering in the fog, and nearer to us, at the foot of the glacis, the Wurtemburg sentinel stood motionless in the poplar alley which leads to the large shed of the tile-kiln.

Everything was still gray and indistinct; though the winter sun, as white as snow, rose above the dark line of firs. Our soldiers stood motionless, with grounded arms, in the covered ways. The "*Verdás!*" and "*Souädas!*" went their rounds. It grew lighter every moment.

No one would have believed that a fight was preparing, when six o'clock sounded from the mayoralty, and suddenly our two companies, without command, started, shouldering their arms; from the covered ways, and silently descended the glacis.

In less than a minute, they reached the road which stretches along the gardens, and defiled to the left, following the hedges.

You cannot imagine my fright when I found that the fight was about to begin. It was not yet clear daylight, but still the enemy's sentinel saw the line of bayonets filing behind the hedges, and called out in a terrible way: "*Verdá!*"

"Forward!" replied Captain Vigneron, in a voice like thunder, and the heavy soles of our soldiers sounded on the hard ground like an avalanche.

The sentinel fired, and then ran up the alley, shouting I know not what. Fifteen of the landwehr, who formed the outpost under the old shed used for drying bricks, started at once; they did not have time for repentance, but were all massacred without mercy.

We could not see very well at that distance, through the hedges and poplars, but after the post was carried, the firing of the musketry and the horrible cries were heard even in the city.

All the unfortunate landwehr who were quartered in the Pernette farm-house—a large number of whom were undressed, like respectable men at home, so as to sleep more comfortably—jumped from the windows in their pantaloons, in their drawers, in their shirts, with t' ir cartridge-boxes on their backs, and ranged themselves behind the tile-kiln, in the large Seltier meadow. Their officers urged them on, and gave their orders in the midst of the tumult.

There must have been six or seven hundred of them there, almost naked in the snow, and, notwithstanding their being thus surprised, they opened a running fire which was well sustained, when our two pieces on the bastion began to take part in the contest.

Oh! what carnage!

Looking down upon them, you should have seen the bullets hit, and the shirts fly in the air! And, what was worst for these poor wretches, they had to close ranks, because, after destroying everything in the tile-kiln, our soldiers went out to make an attack with their bayonets!

What a situation!—just imagine it, Fritz, for respectable citizens, merchants, bankers, brewers, innkeepers—peaceable men who wanted nothing but peace and quietness.

I have always thought, since then, that the landwehr system is a very bad one, and that it is much better to pay a good army of volunteers, who are attached to the country, and know that their pay, pensions, and decorations come from the nation and not from the government; young men devoted to their country like those of '92, and full of enthusiasm, because they are respected and honored in proportion to their sacrifices. Yes, this is what they ought to be—and not men who are thinking of their wives and children.

Our balls struck down these poor fathers and husbands by the dozen. To add to all these abominations, two other companies, sent out with the greatest secrecy by the council of defence from the posterns of the guard and of the German gate, and which came up, one by the Saverne road, and the other by the road of Petit-Saint-Jean, now began to outflank them, and forming behind them, fired upon them in the rear.

It must be confessed that these old soldiers of the Empire had a diabolical talent for stratagem! Who would ever have imagined such a stroke!

On seeing this, the remnant of the landwehr disbanded on the great white plain like a whirlwind of sparrows. Those who had not had time to put on their shoes did not mind the stones or briers or thorns of the Fiquet bottom; they ran like stags, the stoutest as fast as the rest.

Our soldiers followed them as skirmishers, stopping not a second except to make ready and fire. All the ground in front, up to the old beech in the middle of the meadow of Quatre-Vents, was covered with their bodies.

Their colonel, a burgomaster doubtless, galloped before them on horseback, his shirt flying out behind him.

If the Baden soldiers, quartered in the village, had not come to their assistance, they would all have been exterminated. But two battalions of Baden men being deployed at the right of Quatre-Vents, our trumpets sounded the recall, and the four companies formed in the alley *des Dames* to await them.

The Baden soldiers then halted, and the last of the Wurtemburgers passed behind them, glad to escape from such a terrible destruction. They could well say: "I know what war is—I have seen it at the worst!"

It was now seven o'clock—the whole city was on the ramparts. Soon a thick smoke rose above the tile-kiln and the surrounding buildings; some sappers had gone out with faggots and set it on fire,

It was all burned to cinders; nothing remained but a great black space, and some rubbish behind the poplars.

Our four companies, seeing that the Baden soldiers did not mean to attack them, returned quietly, the trumpeter leading.

Long before this, I had gone down to the square, near the German gate, to meet our troops as they came back. It was one of the sights which I shall never forget; the post under arms, the veterans hanging by the chains of the lowered drawbridge; the men, women, and children pushing in the street; and outside, on the ramparts, the trumpets sounding, and answered from the distance, by the echoes of the bastions and half-moon; the wounded, who, pale, tattered, covered with blood, came in first, supported on the shoulders of their comrades; Lieutenant Schnindret, in one of the tile-kiln armchairs, his face covered with sweat, with a bullet in his abdomen, shouting with thick voice and extended hand, "*Vive l'Empereur!*" the soldiers who threw the Wurtemburg commander from his litter to put one of our own in it; the drums under the gate beating the march, while the troops, with arms at will, and bread and all kinds of provisions stuck on their bayonets, entered proudly in the midst of the shouts: "*Hurra for the Sixth Light Infantry!*" These are things which only old people can boast of having seen!

Ah, Fritz, men are not what they once were! In my time, foreigners paid the cost of war. The Emperor Napoleon had that virtue; he ruined not France, but his enemies. Now-a-days we pay for our own glory.

And, in those times, the soldiers brought back booty, sacks, epaulettes, cloaks, officers' sashes, watches, etc., etc.! They remembered that General Bonaparte had said to them in 1796: "You need clothes and shoes; the Republic owes you much, she can give you nothing. I am going to lead you into the richest country in the world; there you will find honors, glory, riches!" In fine, I saw at once that we were going to sell glasses of wine at a great rate.

As the sergeant passed I called to him from the distance, "Sergeant!"

He saw me in the crowd, and we shook hands joyfully. "All right, Father Moses! All right!" he said.

Everybody laughed.

Then, without waiting for the end of the procession, I ran to the market to open my shop.

Little Sâfel had also understood that we were

going to have a profitable day, for, in the midst of the crowd, he had come and pulled my coat-tails, and said, "I have the key of the market; I have it; let us make haste! Let us try to get there before Frichard!"

Whatever natural wit a child may have, it shows itself at once; it is truly a gift of God.

So we ran to the shop. I opened my windows, and Säfel remained while I went home to eat a morsel, and get a good quantity of sous and small change.

Sorlé and Zeffen were at their counter selling small glassfuls. Everything went well as usual. But a quarter of an hour later, when the soldiers had broken ranks and put back their muskets in their places at the barracks, the crowd at my shop in the market, of people wishing to sell me coats, sacks, watches, pistols, cloaks, epaulettes, etc., was so great that without Säfel's help I never could have got out of it.

I got all these things for almost nothing. Men of this sort never trouble themselves about to-morrow; their only thought was to live well from one day to another, to have tobacco, brandy, and the other good things which are never wanting in a garrisoned town.

That day, in six hours' time, I refurnished my

shop with coats, cloaks, pantaloons, and thick boots of genuine German leather, of the first quality, and I bought things of all sorts—nearly fifteen hundred pounds' worth—which I afterward sold for six or seven times more than they cost me. All those landwehr were well-to-do, and even rich citizens, with good, substantial clothes.

The soldiers, too, sold me a good many watches, which Goolden the old watchmaker did not want, because they were taken from the dead.

But what gave me more pleasure than all the rest, was that Frichard, who was sick for three or four days, could not come and open his shop. It makes me laugh now to think of it. It gave the rascal that green jaundice which never left him as long as he lived.

At noon Sâfel went to fetch our dinner in a basket; we ate under the shed so as not to lose custom, and could not leave for a minute till night. Scarcely had one set gone, before two and often three others came at once.

I was sinking with fatigue, and so was Sâfel; nothing but our love of trade sustained us.

Another pleasant thing which I recall is that, on going home a few minutes before seven, we saw at a distance that our other shop was full. My wife and daughter had not been able to close it; they had raised the price, and the soldiers did not even notice it,—it seemed all right to them; so that not only the French money which I had just given them, but also Wurtemburg florins came to my pocket.

Two trades which help each other along are an excellent thing, Fritz: remember that! Without my brandies I should not have had the money to buy so many goods, and without the market where I gave ready money for the booty, the soldiers would not have had wherewith to buy my brandy. This shows us plainly that the Lord favors orderly and peaceable men, provided they know how to make the best use of their opportunities.

At length, as we could not do more, we were obliged to close the shop, in spite of the protestations of the soldiers, and defer business till to-morrow.

About nine o'clock, after supper, we all sat down together around the large lamp, to count our gains. I made rolls of three francs each, and on the chair next me the pile reached almost to the top of the table. Little Sâfel put the white pieces in a wooden bowl. It was a pleasant sight to us all, and Sorlé said: "We have sold twice as much as usual. The more we raise the price the better it sells."

I was going to reply that still we must use moderation in all things—for these women, even the best of them, do not know that—when the sergeant came in to take his little glass. He wore his foraging coat, and carried hung across his cape a kind of bag of red leather.

"He, he, he!" said he, as he saw the rolls. "The devil! the devil! You ought to be satisfied with this day's work, Father Moses?"

"Yes, not bad, sergeant," I joyfully replied.

"I think," said he, as he sat down and tasted the litte glass of cherry-brandy, which Zeffen had just poured out for him, "I think that after one or two sorties more, you will do for colonel of the shopkeepers' regiment. So much the better; I am very glad of it!"

Then, laughing heartily, he said,

"He, Father Moses! see what I have here; these rascals of kaiserlicks deny themselves nothing."

At the same time he opened his bag, and began to draw out a pair of mittens lined with fox-skin, then some good woollen stockings, and a large knife with a horn handle and blades of very fine steel. He opened the blades:

"There is everything here," said he, "a pruning-knife, a saw, small knives and large ones, even to a file for nails."

"For finger-nails, sergeant!" said I.

'Ah! very likely!" said he. "This big landwehr was as nice as a new crown-piece. He would be likely to file his finger-nails. But wait!"

My wife and children, leaning over us, looked on with eager eyes. Thrusting his hand into a sort of portfolio in the side of the bag, he drew out a handsome miniature, surrounded with a circle of gold in the shape of a watch, but larger.

"See! What ought this to be worth?"

I looked, then Sorlé, then Zeffen, and Säfel. We were all surprised at seeing a work of such beauty, and even touched, for the miniature represented a fair young woman and two lovely children, as fresh as rose-buds.

"Well, what do you think of that?" asked the sergeant.

"It is very beautiful," said Sorlé.

"Yes, but what is it worth?"

I took the miniature and examined it.

"To any one else, sergeant," said I, "I should say that it was worth fifty francs; but the gold alone is worth more, and I should estimate it at a hundred francs; we can weigh it."

"And the portrait, Father Moses?"

"The portrait is worth nothing to me, and I will give it back to you. Such things do not sell in this country; they are of no value except to the family.

"Very well," said he, "we will talk about that bye-and-bye."

He put back the miniature into the bag.

"Do you read German?" he asked.

"Very well."

"Ah, good! I am curious to hear what this kaiserlick had to write. See, it is a letter! He was keeping it doubtless for the baggage-master to send it to Germany. But we came too soon! What does it say?"

He handed me a letter addressed to Madame Roedig, Stuttgart, No. 6 Bergstrasse. That letter, Fritz, here it is. Sorlé has kept it; it will tell you more about the landwehr than I can."

"BIEGELBERG, Feb. 25, 1814.

"DEAR AURELIA: Thy good letter of January 29th reached Coblentz too late; the regiment was on its way to Alsace.

"We have had a great many discomforts, from rain and snow. The regiment came first to Bitche, one of the most terrible forts possible, built upon rocks up in the sky. We were to take part in blockading it, but a new order sent us on farther to the fort of Lutzelstein, on the mountain, where we remained two days at the village of Pétersbach, to summon that little place to surrender. The veterans who held it having replied by cannon, our colonel did not judge it necessary to storm it, and, thank God! we received orders to go and blockade another fortress surrounded by good villages which furnish us provisions in abundance; this is Phalsburg, a couple of leagues from Saverne. We relieve, here, the Austrian regiment of Vogelgesang, which has left for Lorraine.

"Thy good letter has followed me everywhere and it fills me now with joy. Embrace little Sabrina and our dear little Henry for me a hundred times, and receive my embraces yourself, too, thou dear, adored wife!

"Ah! when shall we be together again in our little pharmacy? When shall I see again my vials nicely labelled upon their shelves, with the heads of Æsculapius and Hippocrates above the door? When shall I take my pestle, and mix my drugs again after the prescribed formulas? When shall I have the joy of sitting again in my comfortable arm-chair, in front of a good fire, in our back shop, and hear Henry's little wooden horse roll upon the floor,— Henry whom I so long for? And thou, dear, adored wife, when wilt thou exclaim: 'It is my Henry!' as thou seest me return crowned with palms of victory."

"These Germans," interrupted the sergeant, "are

blockheads as well as asses! They are to have 'palms of victory!' What a silly letter!"

But Sorlé and Zeffen listened as I read, with tears in their eyes. They held our little ones in their arms, and I, too, thinking that Baruch might have been in the same condition as this poor man, was greatly moved.

Now, Fritz, hear the end:

'We are here in an old tile-kiln, within range of the cannon of the fort. A few shells are fired upon the city every evening, by order of the Russian general, Berdiaiw, with the hope of making the inhabitants decide to open the gates. That must be before long; they are short of provisions! Then we shall be comfortably lodged in the citizens' houses, till the end of this glorious campaign; and that will be soon, for the regular armies have all passed without resistance, and we hear daily of great victories in Champagne. Bonaparte is in full retreat; field-marshals Blücher and Schwartzenberg have united their forces, and are only five or six days' march from Paris———"

"What? What? What is that? What does he say?" stammered out the sergeant, leaning over toward the letter. "Read that again!"

I looked at him; he was very pale, and his cheeks shook with anger.

"He says that generals Blücher and Schwartzenberg are near Paris."

"Near Paris! They! The rascals!" he faltered out.

Suddenly, with a bad look on his face, he gave a low laugh and said:

"Ah! thou meanest to take Phalsburg, dost thou? Thou meanest to return to thy land of sauerkrout with palms of victory? He! he! he! I have given thee thy palms of victory!"

He made the motions of pricking with his bayonet as he spoke, "One—*two*—hop!"

It made us all tremble only to look at him.

"Yes, Father Moses, so it is," said he, emptying his glass by little sips. "I have nailed this sort of an apothecary to the door of the tile-kiln. He made up a funny face—his eyes starting from his head. His Aurelia will have to expect him a good while! But never mind! Only, Madame Sorlé, I assure you that it is a lie. You must not believe a word he says. The Emperor will give it to them! Don't be troubled."

I did not wish to go on. I felt myself grow cold, and I finished the letter quickly, passing over three-quarters of it which contained no information, only compliments for friends and acquaintances.

The sergeant himself had had enough of it, and

went out soon afterward, saying, "Good-night! Throw that in the fire!"

Then I put the letter aside, and we all sat looking at each other for some minutes. I opened the door. The sergeant was in his room at the end of the passage, and I said, in a low voice:

"What a horrible thing! Not only to kill the father of a family like a fly, but to laugh about it afterward!"

"Yes," replied Sorlé. "And the worst of it is that he is not a bad man. He loves the Emperor too well, that is all!"

The information contained in the letter caused us much serious reflection, and that night, notwithstanding our stroke of good fortune in our sales, I woke more than once, and thought of this terrible war, and wondered what would become of the country if Napoleon were no longer its master. But these questions were above my comprehension, and I did not know how to answer them.

XVII.

FAMINE AND FEVER.

After this story of the landwehr, we were afraid of the sergeant, though he did not know it, and came regularly to take his glass of cherry-brandy. Sometimes in the evening he would hold the bottle before our lamp, and exclaim:

"It is getting low, Father Moses, it is getting low! We shall soon be put upon half-rations, and then quarter, and so on. It is all the same; if a drop is left, anything more than the smell, in six months, Trubert will be very glad."

He laughed, and I thought with indignation:

"You will be satisfied with a drop! What are you in want of? The city storehouses are bomb-proof, the fires at the guard-house are burning every day, the market furnishes every soldier with his ration of fresh meat, while respectable citizens are glad if they can get potatoes and salt meat!"

This is the way I felt in my ill-humor, while I treated him pleasantly, all the same, on account of his terrible wickedness.

And it was the truth, Fritz, even our children had nothing more nourishing to eat than soup made of potatoes and salt beef, which cause many dangerous maladies.

The garrison had no lack of anything; but, notwithstanding, the governor was all the time proclaiming that the visits were to be recommenced, and that those who should be found delinquent should be punished with the rigor of military law. Those people wanted to have everything for themselves; but nobody minded them, everybody hid what he could.

Fortunate in those times was he who kept a cow in his cellar, with some hay and straw for fodder; milk and butter were beyond all price. Fortunate was he who owned a few hens; a fresh egg, at the end of February, was valued at fifteen sous, and they were not to be had even at that price. The price of fresh meat went up, so to speak, from hour to hour, and we did not ask if it was beef or horse-flesh.

The council of defence had sent away the paupers of the city before the blockade, but a large number of poor people remained. A good many slipped out at night into the trenches by one of the posterns; they would go and dig up roots from under the snow, and cut the nettles in the bastions to boil for spinage. The sentries fired from above, but what will not a man risk for food? It is better to feel a ball than to suffer with hunger.

We needed only to meet these emaciated creatures, these women dragging themselves along the walls, these pitiful children, to feel that famine had come, and we often said to ourselves:

"If the Emperor does not come and help us, in a month we shall be like these wretched creatures! What good will our money do us, when a raddish will cost a hundred francs?"

Then, Fritz, we smiled no more as we saw the little ones eating around the table; we looked at each other, and this glance was enough to make us understand each other.

The good sense and good feeling of a brave woman are seen at times like this. Sorlé had never spoken to me about our provisions; I knew how prudent she was, and supposed that we must have provisions hidden somewhere, without being entirely sure of it. So, at evening, as we sat at our meagre supper, the fear that our children might want the necessary food sometimes led me to say:

"Eat! feast away! I am not hungry. I want

an omelet or a chicken. Potatoes do not agree with me."

I would laugh, but Sorlé knew very well what I was thinking.

"Come, Moses," she said to me one day; "we are not as badly off as you think; and if we should come to it, ah, well! do not be troubled, we shall find some way of getting along! So long as others have something to live upon, we shall not perish, more than they."

She gave me courage, and I ate cheerfully, I had so much confidence in her.

That same evening, after Zeffen and the children had gone to bed, Sorlé took the lamp, and led me to her hiding-place.

Under the house we had three cellars, very small and very low, separated by lattices. Against the last of these lattices, Sorlé had thrown bundles of straw up to the very top; but after removing the straw, we went in, and I saw at the further end, two bags of potatoes, a bag of flour, and on the little oil-cask a large piece of salt beef.

We stayed there more than an hour, to look, and calculate, and think. These provisions might serve us for a month, and those in the large cellar under the street, which we had declared to the commissary of provisions, a fortnight. So that Sorlé said to me as we went up :

"You see that, with economy, we have what will do for six weeks. A time of great want is now beginning, and if the Emperor does not come before the end of six weeks, the city will surrender. Meanwhile, we must get along with potatoes and salt meat."

She was right, but every day I saw how the children were suffering from this diet. We could see that they grew thin, especially little David; his large bright eyes, his hollow cheeks, his increasing dejected look, made my heart ache.

I held him, I caressed him; I whispered to him that, when the winter was over, we would go to Saverne, and his father would take him to drive in his carriage. He would look at me dreamily, and then lay his head upon my shoulder, with his arm around my neck, without answering. At last he refused to eat.

Zeffen, too, became disheartened; she would often sob, and take her babe from me, and say that she wanted to go, that she wanted to see Baruch! You do not know what these troubles are, Fritz; a father's troubles for his children; they are the cruelest of all! No child can imagine how his parents love him, and what they suffer when he is unhappy.

But what was to be done in the midst of such

calamities? Many other families in France were still more to be pitied than we.

During all this time, you must remember that we had the patrols, the shells in the evening, requisition and notices, the call to arms at the two barracks and in front of the mayoralty, the cries of "Fire!" in the night, the noise of the fire-engines, the arrival of the envoys, the rumors spread through the city that our armies were retreating, and that the city was to be burned to the ground!

The less people know the more they invent.

It is best to tell the simple truth. Then every one would take courage, for, during all such times, I have always seen that the truth, even in the greatest calamities, is never so terrible as these inventions. The republicans defended themselves so well, because they knew everything, nothing was concealed from them, and every one considered the affairs of his nation as his own.

But when men's own affairs are hidden from them, how can they have confidence? An honest man has nothing to conceal, and I say it is the same with an honest government.

In short, bad weather, cold, want, rumors of all kinds, increased our miseries. Men like Burguet, whom we had always seen firm, became sad; all that they could say to us was:

"We shall see!—we must wait!" The soldiers again began to desert, and were shot!

Our brandy-selling always kept on: I had already emptied seven pipes of spirit, all my debts were paid, my store-house at the market was full of goods, and I had eighteen thousand francs in the cellar; but what is money, when we are trembling for the life of those we love?

On the sixth of March, about nine o'clock in the evening, we had just finished supper as usual, and the sergeant was smoking his pipe, with his legs crossed, near the window, and looking at us without speaking.

It was the hour when the bombarding began; we heard the first cannon-shots, behind the Fiquet bottom-land; a cannon-shot from the outposts had answered them; that had somewhat roused us, for we were all thoughtful.

"Father Moses," said the sergeant, "the children are pale!"

"I know it very well,' I replied, sorrowfully.

He said no more, and as Zeffen had just gone out to weep, he took little David on his knee, and looked at him for a long time. Sorlé held little Esdras asleep in her arms. Säfel took off the tablecloth and rolled up the napkins, to put them back in the closet.

"Yes," said the sergeant. "We must take care, Father Moses; we will talk about it another time."

I looked at him with surprise; he emptied his pipe at the edge of the stove, and went out, making a sign for me to follow him. Zeffen came in, and I took a candle from her hand. The sergeant led me to his little room at the end of the passage, shut the door, sat down on the foot of the bed, and said:

"Father Moses, do not be frightened—but the typhus has just broken out again in the city; five soldiers were taken to the hospital this morning; the commandant of the place, Moulin, is taken. I hear, too, of a woman and three children!"

He looked at me, and I felt cold all over.

"Yes," said he, "I have known this disease for a long time; we had it in Poland, in Russia, after the retreat, and in Germany. It always comes from poor nourishment."

Then I could not help sobbing and exclaiming:

"Ah, tell me! What can I do? If I could give my life for my children, it would all be well! But what can I do?"

"To-morrow, Father Moses, I will bring you my portion of meat, and you shall have soup made of it for your children. Madame Sorlé may take the piece at the market, or, if you prefer, I will bring it myself. You shall have all my portions of fresh meat till the blockade is over, Father Moses."

I was so moved by this, that I went to him and took his hand, saying:

"Sergeant, you are a noble man! Forgive me, I have thought evil of you."

"What about?" said he, scowling.

"About the landwehr at the tile-kiln!"

"Ah, good! That is a different thing! I do not care about that," said he. "If you knew all the *kaiserlichs* that I have dispatched these ten years, you would have thought more evil of me. But that is not what we are talking about; you accept, Father Moses?"

"And you, sergeant," said I, "what will you have to eat?"

"Do not be troubled about that; Sergeant Trubert has never been in want!"

I wanted to thank him. "Good!" said he, "that is all understood. I cannot give you a pike, or a fat goose, but a good soup in blockade times is worth something, too."

He laughed and shook hands with me. As for myself I was quite overcome, and my eyes were full of tears.

"Let us go; good-night!" said he, as he led me to the door. "It will all come out right! Tell Madame Sorlé that it will all come out right!"

I blessed that man as I went out, and I told it all to Sorlé, who was still more affected by it than myself. We could not refuse; it was for the children! and during the last week there had been nothing but horse-meat in the market.

So the next morning we had fresh meat to make soup for those poor little ones. But the dreadful malady was already upon us, Fritz! Now, when I think of it, after all these years, I am quite overcome. However, I cannot complain; before going to take the bit of meat, I had consulted our old rabbi about the quality of this meat according to the law, and he had replied:

"The first law is to save Israel; but how can Israel be saved if the children perish?"

But after a while I remembered that other law:

"The life of the flesh is in the blood, therefore I said unto the children of Israel: Ye shall eat the blood of no manner of flesh, for the life of all flesh is the blood thereof; whosoever eateth it shall be cut off; and whosoever eateth of any sick beast shall be unclean."

In my great misery the words of the Lord came to me, and I wept.

All these animals had been sick for six weeks; they lived in the mire, exposed to the snow and wind, between the arsenal and guard bastions.

The soldiers, almost all of whom were sons of peasants, ought to have known that they could not live in the open air, in such cold weather; a shelter could easily have been made. But when officers take the whole charge, nobody else thinks of anything; they even forget their own village trades. And if, unfortunately, their commanders do not give the order, nothing is done.

This is the reason that the animals had neither flesh nor fat; this is the reason that they were nothing but miserable, trembling carcasses, and their suffering, unhealthy flesh had become unclean, according to the law of God.

Many of the soldiers died. The wind brought to the city the bad air from the bodies, scattered by hundreds around the tile-kiln, the Ozillo farm, and in the gardens, and this also caused much sickness.

The justice of the Lord is shown in all things; when the living neglect their duties toward the dead, they perish.

I have often remembered these things when it was too late, so that I think of them only with grief.

XVIII.

DEATH OF LITTLE DAVID.

The most painful of all my recollections, Fritz, is the way in which that terrible disease came to our family.

On the twelfth of March we heard of a large number of men, women, and children who were dying. We dared not listen; we said:

"No one in our house is sick, the Lord watches over us!"

After David had come, after supper, to cuddle in my arms, with his little hand on my shoulder, I looked at him; he seemed very drowsy, but children are always sleepy at night. Esdras was already asleep, and Säfel had just bidden us good-night.

At last Zeffen took the child, and we all went to bed.

That night the Russians did not fire; perhaps the typhus was among them, too. I do not know.

About midnight, when by God's goodness we were asleep, I heard a terrible cry.

I listened, and Sorlé said to me:

"It is Zeffen!"

I rose at once, and tried to light the lamp; but I was so much agitated that I could not find anything.

Sorlé struck a light, I drew on my pantaloons and ran to the door. But I was hardly in the passageway when Zeffen came out of her room like an insane person, with her long black hair all loose.

"The child!" she screamed.

Sorlé followed me. We went in, we leaned over the cradle. The two children seemed to be sleeping; Esdras all rosy, David as white as snow.

At first I saw nothing, I was so frightened, but at last I took up David to waken him; I shook him, and called, "David!"

And then we first saw that his eyes were open and fixed.

"Wake him! wake him!" cried Zeffen.

Sorlé took my hands and said:

"Quick! make a fire! heat some water!"

And we laid him across the bed, shaking him and calling him by name. Little Esdras began to cry.

"Light a fire!" said Sorlé again to me. "And, Zeffen, be quiet! It does no good to cry so! Quick, quick, a fire!"

But Zeffen cried out incessantly, "My poor child!"

"He will soon be warm again," said Sorlé; "only, Moses, make haste and dress yourself, and run for Doctor Steinbrenner."

She was pale and more alarmed than we, but this brave woman never lost her presence of mind or her courage. She had made a fire, and the faggots were crackling in the chimney.

I ran to get my cloak, and went down, thinking to myself:

"The Lord have mercy upon us! If the child dies I shall not survive him! No, he is the one that I love best, I could not survive him!"

For you know, Fritz, that the child who is most unhappy, or in the greatest danger, is always the one that we love best; he needs us the most; we forget the others. The Lord has ordered it so, doubtless for the greatest good.

I was already running in the street.

A darker night was never known. The wind blew from the Rhine, the snow blew about like dust; here and there the lighted windows showed where people were watching the sick.

My head was uncovered, yet I did not feel the cold. I cried within myself:

"The last day had come! That day of which the Lord has said: 'Afore the harvest, when the bud is perfect, and the sour grape is ripening in the flower, he shall both cut off the sprigs with pruning-hooks, and take away and cut down the branches.'"

Full of these fearful thoughts, I went across the large market-place, where the wind was tossing the old elms, full of frost.

As the clock struck one, I pushed open Doctor Steinbrenner's door; its large pulley rattled in the vestibule. As I was groping about, trying to find the railing, the servant appeared with a light at the top of the stairs.

"Who is there?" she asked, holding the lantern before her.

"Ah!" I replied, "tell the doctor to come immediately; we have a child sick, very sick."

I could not restrain my sobs.

"Come up, Monsieur Moses," said the girl: "the doctor has just come in, and has not gone to bed. Come up a moment and warm yourself!"

But Father Steinbrenner had heard it all.

"Very well, Theresa!" said he, coming out of his room; "keep the fire burning. I shall be back in an hour at latest."

He had already put on his large three-cornered cap, and his goat's-hair great-coat.

We walked across the square without speaking. I went first; in a few minutes we ascended our stairs

Sorlé had placed a candle at the top of the stairs, I took it and led M. Steinbrenner to the baby's room.

All seemed quiet as we entered. Zeffen was sitting in an arm-chair behind the door, with her head on her knees, and her shoulders uncovered; she was no longer crying but weeping. The child was in bed. Sorlé, standing at its side, looked at us.

The doctor laid his cap on the bureau.

"It is too warm here," said he, "give us a little air."

Then he went to the bed. Zeffen had risen from her chair, as pale as death. The doctor took the lamp, and looked at our poor little David; he raised the coverlet and lifted out the little round limbs; he listened to the breathing. Esdras having begun to cry, he turned round and said: "Take the other child away from this room—we must be quiet! and besides, the air of a sick-room is not good for such small children."

He gave me a side look. I understood what he meant to say. It was the typhus! I looked at my wife; she understood it all.

I felt at that moment as if my heart were torn; I wanted to groan, but Zeffen was there leaning over, behind us, and I said nothing; nor did Sorlé.

The doctor asked for paper to write a prescription,

and we went out together. I led him to our room, and shut the door, and began to sob.

"Moses," said he, "you are a man, do not weep! Remember that you ought to set an example of courage to two poor women."

"Is there no hope?" I asked him in a low voice, afraid of being heard.

"It is the typhus!" said he. "We will do what we can. There, that is the prescription; go to Tribolin's; his boy is up at night now, and he will give you the medicine. Be quick! And then, in heaven's name, take the other child out of that room, and your daughter too, if possible. Try to find some one out of the family, accustomed to sickness; the typhus is contagious."

I said nothing.

He took his cap and went.

Now what can I say more? The typhus is a disease engendered by death itself; the prophet speaks of it, when he says:

"Hell from beneath is moved for thee, to meet thee at thy coming!"

How many have I seen die of the typhus in our hospitals, on the Saverne hill, and elsewhere!

When men tear each other to pieces, without mercy, why should not death come to help them? But what had this poor babe done that it must die so soon? This, Fritz, is the most dreadful thing, that all must suffer for the crimes of a few. Yes, when I think that my child died of this pestilence, which war had brought from the heart of Russia to our homes, and which ravaged all Alsace and Lorraine for six months, instead of accusing God, as the impious do, I accuse men. Has not God given them reason? And when they do not use it—when they let themselves rage against each other like brutes— is He to blame for it?

But of what use are right ideas, when we are suffering!

I remember that the sickness lasted for six days, and those were the cruelest days of my life. I feared for my wife, for my daughter, for Säfel, for Esdras. I sat in a corner, listening to the babe's breathing. Sometimes he seemed to breathe no longer. Then a chill passed over me; I went to him and listened. And when, by chance, Zeffen came, in spite of the doctor's prohibition, I went into a sort of fury; I pushed her out by the shoulders, trembling.

"But he is my child! He is my child!" she said.

"And art thou not my child too?" said I. "I do not want you all to die!"

Then I burst into tears, and fell into my chair,

looking straight before me, my strength all gone; I was exhausted with grief.

Sorlé came and went, with firm-closed lips; she prepared everything, and cared for everybody.

At that time musk was the remedy for typhus; the house was full of musk. Often the idea seized me that Esdras, too, was going to be sick. Ah, if having children is the greatest happiness in the world, what agony is it to see them suffer! How fearful to think of losing them!—to be there, to hear their labored breathing, their delirium, to watch their sinking from hour to hour, from minute to minute, and to exclaim from the depths of the soul:

"Death is near at hand! There is nothing, nothing more that can be done to save thee, my child! I cannot give thee my life! Death does not wish for it!"

What heart-rending and what anguish, till the last moment when all is over!

Then, Fritz, money, the blockade, the famine, the general desolation—all were forgotten. I hardly saw the sergeant open our door every morning, and look in, asking:

"Well, Father Moses, well?"

I did not know what he said; I paid no attention to him.

But, what I always think of with pleasure, what I am always proud of, is that, in the midst of all this trouble, when Sorlé, Zeffen, myself, and everybody were beside ourselves, when we forgot all about our business, and let everything go, little Sâfel at once took charge of our shop. Every morning we heard him rise at six o'clock, go down, open the warehouse, take up one or two pitchers of brandy, and begin to serve the customers.

No one had said a word to him about it, but Sâfel had a genius for trade. And if anything could console a father in such troubles, it would be to see himself, as it were, living over again in so young a child, and to say to himself: "At least the good race is not extinct; it still remains to preserve common-sense in the world." Yes, it is the only consolation which a man can have.

Our *schabes goïe* did the work in the kitchen, and old Lanche helped us watch, but Sâfel took the charge of the shop; his mother and I thought of nothing but our little David.

He died in the night of the eighteenth of March, the day when the fire broke out in Captain Cabanier's house.

That same night two shells fell upon our house; the blindage made them roll into the court, where they both burst, shattering the laundry windows and demolishing the butcher's door, which fell down at once with a fearful crash.

It was the most powerful bombardment since the blockade began, for, as soon as the enemy saw the flame ascending, they fired from Mittelbronn, from the Barracks, and the Fiquet lowlands, to prevent its being extinguished.

I stayed all the while with Sorlé, near the babe's bed, and the noise of the bursting shells did not disturb us.

The unhappy do not cling to life, and then the child was so sick! There were blue spots all over his body.

The end was drawing near.

I walked the room. Without they were crying "Fire! Fire!"

People passed in the street like a torrent. We heard those returning from the fire telling the news, the engines hurrying by, the soldiers ranging the crowd in the line, the shells bursting at the right and left.

Before our windows the long trails of red flame descended upon the roofs in front, and shattered the glass of the windows. Our cannon all around the city replied to the enemy. Now and then we heard the cry: "Room! Room!" as the wounded were carried away.

Twice some pickets came up into my room to put me in the line, but, on seeing me sitting with Sorlé by our child, they went down again.

The first shell burst at our house about eleven o'clock, the second at four in the morning; everything shook, from the garret to the cellar; the floor, the bed, the furniture seemed to be upheaved; but, in our exhaustion and despair, we did not speak a single word.

Zeffen came running to us with Esdras and little Sâfel, at the first explosion. It was evident that little David was dying. Old Lanche and Sorlé were sitting, sobbing. Zeffen began to cry.

I opened the windows wide, to admit the air, and the powder-smoke which covered the city came into the room.

Sâfel saw at once that the hour was at hand. I needed only to look at him, and he went out, and soon returned by a side street, notwithstanding the crowd, with Kalmes the chanter, who began to recite the prayer of the dying:

"The Lord reigneth! The Lord reigneth! The Lord shall reign everywhere and forever!

"Praise, everywhere and forever, the name of his glorious reign!

"The Lord is God! The Lord is God! The Lord is God!

"Hear, oh Israel, the Lord our God is one God!

"Go, then, where the Lord calleth thee—go, and may his mercy help thee!

"May the Lord, our God, be with thee; may his immortal angels lead thee to heaven, and may the righteous be glad when the Lord shall receive thee into his bosom!

"God of mercy, receive this soul into the midst of eternal joys!"

Sorlé and I repeated, weeping, those holy words. Zeffen lay as if dead, her arms extended across the bed, over the feet of her child. Her brother Sâfel stood behind her, weeping bitterly, and calling softly, "Zeffen! Zeffen!"

But she did not hear; her soul was lost in infinite sorrows.

Without, the cries of "Fire!" the orders for the engines, the tumult of the crowd, the rolling of the cannonade still continued; the flashes, one after another, lighted up the darkness.

What a night, Fritz! What a night!

Suddenly Sâfel, who was leaning over under the curtain, turned round to us in terror. My wife and I ran, and saw that the child was dead. We raised our hands, sobbing, to indicate it. The chanter ceased his psalm. Our David was dead!

The most terrible thing was the mother's cry! She

lay, stretched out, as if she had fainted; but when the chanter leaned over and closed the lips, saying "*Amen!*" she rose, lifted the little one, looked at him, then, raising him above her head, began to run toward the door, crying out with a heart-rending voice:

"Baruch! Baruch! save our child!"

She was mad, Fritz! In this last terror I stopped her, and, by main force, took from her the little body which she was carrying away. And Sorlé, throwing her arms round her, with ceaseless groanings, Mother Lanche, the chanter, Sâfel, all led her away.

I remained alone, and I heard them go down, leading away my daughter.

How can a man endure such sorrows?

I put David back in the bed and covered him, because of the open windows. I knew that he was dead, but it seemed to me as if he would be cold. I looked at him for a long time, so as to retain that beautiful face in my heart.

It was all heart-rending—all! I felt as if my bowels were torn from me, and in my madness I accused the Lord, and said:

"I am the man that hath seen affliction by the rod of thy wrath. Surely against me is he turned. My flesh and my skin hath he made old: he hath

"BARUCH! BARUCH! SAVE OUR CHILD."

broken my bones. He hath set me in dark places. Also when I cry and shout he shutteth out my prayer. He was unto me as a lion in secret places!"

Thus I walked about, groaning and even blaspheming. But God in his mercy forgave me; he knew that it was not myself that spoke, but my despair.

At last I sat down, the others came back. Sorlé sat next to me in silence. Sâfel said to me:

"Zeffen has gone to the rabbi's with Esdras."

I covered my head without answering him.

Then some women came with old Lanche; I took Sorlé by the hand, and we went into the large room, without speaking a word.

The mere sight of this room, where the two little brothers had played so long, made my tears come afresh, and Sorlé, Sâfel, and I wept together. The house was full of people; it might have been eight o'clock, and they knew already that we had a child **dead.**

XIX.

THE PASSOVER.

Then, Fritz, the funeral rites began. All who died of typhus had to be buried the same day: Christians behind the church, and Jews in the trenches, in the place now occupied by the riding-school.

Old women were already there to wash the poor little body, and comb the hair, and cut the nails, according to the law of the Lord. Some of them sewed the winding-sheet.

The open windows admitted the air, the shutters struck against the walls. The *schamess** went through the streets, striking the doors with his mace, to summon our brethren.

Sorlé sat upon the ground with her head veiled. Hearing Desmarets come up the stairs, I had courage to go and meet him, and show him the

---

* Beadle.

room. The poor angel was in his little shirt on the floor, the head raised a little on some straw, and the little *thaleth* in his fingers. He was so beautiful, with his brown hair, and half-opened lips, that I thought as I looked at him: "The Lord wanted to have thee near his throne!"

And my tears fell silently: my beard was full of them.

Desmarets then took the measure and went. Half an hour afterward, he returned with the little pine coffin under his arm, and the house was filled anew with lamentations.

I could not see the coffin closed! I went and sat upon the sack of ashes, covering my face with both hands, and crying in my heart like Jacob, "Surely I shall go down to the grave with this child; I shall not survive him."

Only a very few of our brethren came, for a panic was in the city; men knew that the angel of death was passing by, and that drops of blood rained from his sword upon the houses; each emptied the water from his jug upon the threshold and entered quickly. But the best of them came silently, and as evening approached, it was necessary to go and descend by the postern.

I was the only one of our family. Sorlé was not able to follow me, nor Zeffen. I was the only one to throw the shovelful of earth. My strength all left me, they had to lead me back to our door. The sergeant held me by the arm; he spoke to me and I did not hear him; I was as if dead.

All else that I remember of that dreadful day, is the moment when, having come into the house, sitting on the sack, before our cold hearth, with bare feet and bent head, and my soul in the depths, the *schamess* came to me, touched my shoulder and made me rise; and then took his knife from his pocket and rent my garment, tearing it to the hip This blow was the last and the most dreadful; I fell back, murmuring with Job:

"Let the day perish wherein I was born, and the night in which it was said, there is a man child conceived! Let a cloud dwell upon it, let the blackness of the day terrify it! For mourning, the true mourning does not come down from the father to the child, but goes up from the child to the father. Why did the knees prevent me? or why the breasts that I should suck? For now I should have lain still in the tomb and been at rest!"

And my grief, Fritz, had no bounds; "What will Baruch say," I exclaimed, "and what shall I answer him when he asks me to give him back his child?"

I felt no longer any interest in our business. Zeffen lived with the old rabbi; her mother spent the days with her, to take care of Esdras and comfort her.

Every part of our house was opened; the *schabes goïe* burned sugar and spices, and the air from without had free circulation. Säfel went on selling.

As for myself, I sat before the hearth in the morning, cooked some potatoes, and ate them with a little salt, and then went out, without thought or aim. I wandered sometimes to the right, sometimes to the left, toward the old gen-d'armery, around the ramparts, in out-of-the-way places.

I could not bear to see any one, especially those who had known the child.

Then, Fritz, our miseries were at their height; famine, cold, all kinds of sufferings weighed upon the city; faces grew thin, and women and children were seen, half-naked and trembling, groping in the shadow in the deserted by-ways.

Ah! such miseries will never return! We have no more such abominable wars, lasting twenty years, when the highways looked like ruts, and the roads like streams of mud; when the ground remained untilled for want of husbandmen, when houses sank for want of inhabitants; when the poor went barefoot and the rich in wooden shoes, while the superior officers passed by on superb horses, looking down contemptuously on the whole human race

We could not endure that now!

But at that time everything in the nation was destroyed and humiliated; the citizens and the people had nothing left; force was everything. If a man said, "But there is such a thing as justice, right, truth!" the way was to answer with a smile, "I do not understand you!" and you were taken for a man of sense and experience, who would make his way.

Then, in the midst of my sorrow, I saw these things without thinking about them; but since then they have come back to me, and thousands of others; all the survivors of those days can remember them, too.

One morning, I was under the old market, looking at the wretches as they bought meat. At that time they knocked down the horses of Rouge-Colas and those of the gendarmes, as fleshless as the cattle in the trenches, and sold the meat at very high prices.

I looked at the swarms of wrinkled old women, of hollow-eyed citizens, all these wretched creatures crowding before Frantz Sépel's stall, while he distributed bits of carcass to them.

Frantz's large dogs were seen no longer prowling about the market, licking up the bloody scraps. The dried hands of old women were stretched out at the end of their fleshless arms, to snatch everything; weak voices called out entreatingly, "A little more liver, Monsieur Frantz, so that we can make merry!"

I saw all this under the great dark roof, through which a little light came, in the holes made by the shells. In the distance, among the worm-eaten pillars, some soldiers, under the arch of the guard house, with their old capes hanging down their thighs, were also looking on;—it seemed like a dream.

My great sorrow accorded with these sad sights. I was about leaving at the end of a half hour, when I saw Burguet coming along by Father Brainstein's old country-house, which was now staved in by the shells, and leaning, all shattered, over the street.

Burguet had told me several days before our affliction, that his maid-servant was sick. I had thought no more of it, but now it came to me.

He looked so changed, so thin, his cheeks so marked by wrinkles, it seemed as if years had passed since I had seen him. His hat came down to his eyes, and his beard, at least a fortnight old, had turned gray. He came in, looking round in all directions; but he could not see me where I was, in the deep shadow, against the planks of the old fodder-house; and he stopped behind the crowd of old women, who were squeezed in a semicircle before the stall, awaiting their turn.

After a minute he put some sous in Frantz Sépel's hand, and received his morsel, which he hid under his cloak. Then looking round again, he was going away quickly, with his head down.

This sight moved my heart: I hurried away, raising my hands to heaven, and exclaiming; "Is it possible? Is it possible? Burguet too! A man of his genius to suffer hunger and eat carcasses! Oh, what times of trial!"

I went home, completely upset.

We had not many provisions left; but, still, the next morning, as Sâfel was going down to open the shop, I said to him:

"Stop, my child, take this little basket to M. Burguet; it is some potatoes and salt beef. Take care that nobody sees it, they would take it from you. Say that it is in remembrance of the poor deserter."

The child went. He told me that Burguet wept.

This, Fritz, is what must be seen in a blockade, where you are attacked from day to day. This is what the Germans and Spaniards had to suffer, and what we suffered in our turn. This is war!

Even the siege rations were almost gone; but Moulin, the commandant of the place, having died of typhus, the famine did not prevent the lieutenant-colonel, who took his place, from giving balls and fêtes to the envoys, in the old Thévenot house. The windows were bright, music played, the staff-officers drank punch and warm wine, to make believe that we were living in abundance. There was good reason for bandaging the eyes of these envoys till they reached the very ball-room, for, if they had seen the look of the people, all the punch-bowls and warm wines in the world would not have deceived them.

All this time, the grave-digger Mouyot and his two boys came every morning to take their two or three drops of brandy. They might say "We drink to the dead!" as the veterans said "We drink to the Cossacks!" Nobody in the city would willingly have undertaken to bury those who had died of typhus; they alone, after taking their drop, dared to throw the bodies from the hospital upon a cart, and pile them up in the pit, and then they passed for grave-diggers, with father Zébédé.

The order was to wrap the dead in a sheet. But who saw that it was done? Old Mouyot himself told me that they were buried in their cloaks or vests, as it might be, and sometimes entirely naked.

For every corpse, these men had their thirty-five sous; Father Mouyot, the blind man, can tell you so; it was his harvest.

Toward the end of March, in the midst of this fearful want, when there was not a dog, and still less a cat, to be seen in the streets, the city was full of evil tidings; rumors of battles lost, of marches upon Paris, etc.

As the envoys had been received, and balls given in their honor, something of our misfortunes became known either through the family or the servants.

Often, in wandering through the streets which ran along the ramparts, I mounted one of the bastions, looking toward Strasburg, or Metz, or Paris. I had no fear then of stray balls. I looked forth upon the thousand bivouac fires scattered over the plain, the soldiers of the enemy returning from the villages with their long poles hung with quarters of meat, at others crouched around the little fires which shone like stars upon the edge of the forest, and at their patrols and their covered batteries from which their flag was flying.

Sometimes I looked at the smoke of the chimneys at Quatre-Vents, or Bibelberg, or Mittelbronn. Our chimneys had no smoke, our festive days were over.

You can never imagine how many thoughts come to you, when you are so shut up, as your eyes follow the long white highways, and you imagine yourself walking there, talking with people about the news, asking them what they have suffered, and telling them what you have yourself endured.

From the bastion of the guard, I could see even the white peaks of the Schneeberg; I imagined myself in the midst of foresters, wood-cutters, and wood-splitters. There was a rumor that they were defending their route from Schirmeck; I longed to know if it were true.

As I looked toward the Maisons-Rouges, on the road to Paris, I imagined myself to be with my old friend Leiser; I saw him at his hearth, in despair at having to support so many people, for the Russian, Austrian, and Bavarian staff-officers remained upon this route, and new regiments went by continually.

And spring came! The snow began to melt in the furrows and behind the hedges. The great forests of La Bonne Fontaine and the Barracks began to change their tints.

The thing which affected me most, as I have often remembered, was hearing the first lark at the end of March. The sky was entirely clear, and I looked up to see the bird. I thought of little David, and I wept, I knew not why.

Men have strange thoughts; they are affected by the song of a bird, and sometimes, years after, the same sounds recall the same emotions, so as even to make them weep.

At last the house was purified, and Zeffen and Sorlé came back to it.

The time of the Passover drew near; and the doors must be washed, the walls scoured, the vessels cleansed. In the midst of these cares, the poor women forgot, in some measure, our affliction; but as the time drew nearer our anxiety increased; how, in the midst of this famine, were we to obey the command of God:

"This month shall be the first month of the year to you.

"In the tenth day of this month they shall take to them every man a lamb, according to the house of their fathers, a lamb for a house.

"Ye shall take it out from the sheep or from the goats.

"And ye shall keep it until the fourteenth day of the same month.

"And they shall eat the flesh in that night, roast with fire, and unleavened bread; and with bitter herbs shall they eat it."

But where was the sacrificial lamb to be found? Schmoûlé alone, the old *schamess*, had thought of it for us all, three months before; he had nourished a male goat of that year in his cellar, and that was the goat that was killed.

Every Jewish family had a portion of it, small indeed, but the law of the Lord was fulfilled.

We invited on that day, according to the law, one of the poorest of our brethren, Kalmes. We went together to the synagogue; the prayers were recited, and then we returned to partake of the feast at our table.

Everything was ready and according to the proper order, notwithstanding the great destitution; the white cloth, the goblet of vinegar, the hard egg, the horseradish, the unleavened bread, and the flesh of the goat. The lamp with seven burners shone above it; but we had not much bread.

Having taken my seat in the midst of my family, Säfel took the jug and poured water upon my hands; then we all bent forward, each took a piece of bread, saying with heavy hearts:

"This is the bread of affliction which our fathers ate in Egypt. Whosoever is hungry, let him come and eat with us. Whosoever is poor, let him come and make the Passover!"

We sat down again, and Säfel said to me:

"What mean ye by this service, my father?"

And I answered:

"We were slaves in Egypt, my child, and the Lord brought us forth with a mighty hand and an outstretched arm!"

These words inspired us with courage; we hoped that God would deliver us as he had delivered our fathers, and that the Emperor would be his right arm; but we were mistaken; the Lord wanted nothing more of that man!

XX.

PEACE.

The next morning, at daybreak, between six and seven o'clock, when we were all asleep, the report of a cannon made our windows rattle. The enemy usually fired only at night. I listened; a second report followed after a few seconds, then another, then others, one by one.

I rose, opened a window, and looked out. The sun was rising behind the arsenal. Not a soul was in the street; but, as one report came after another, doors and windows were opened; men in their shirts leaned out, listening.

No shells hissed through the air; the enemy fired blank cartridges.

As I listened, a great murmur came from the distance, outside of the city. First it came from the Mittelbronn hill, then it reached the Bibelberg, Quatre-Vents, the upper and lower Barracks.

Sorlé had just risen also; I finished dressing, and said to her:

"Something extraordinary is going on—God grant that it may be for good!"

And I went down in great perturbation.

It was not a quarter of an hour since the first report, and the whole city was out. Some ran to the ramparts, others were in groups, shouting and disputing at the corners of the streets. Astonishment, fear, and anger were depicted upon every face.

A large number of soldiers were mingled with the citizens, and all went up together in groups to the right and left of the French gate.

I was about following one of these groups, when Burguet came down the street. He looked thin and emaciated, as on the day when I saw him in the market.

"Well!" said I, running to meet him, "this is something serious!"

"Very serious, and promising no good, Moses!" said he.

"Yes, it is evident," said I, "that the allies have gained victories; it may be that they are in Paris!"

He turned around in alarm, and said in a low voice:

"Take care, Moses, take care! If any one heard

you, at a moment like this, the veterans would tear you in pieces!"

I was dreadfully frightened, for I saw that he was right, while, as for him, his cheeks shook. He took me by the arm and said:

"I owe you thanks for the provisions you sent me; they came very opportunely."

And when I answered that we should always have a morsel of bread at his service, so long as we had any left, he pressed my hand; and we went together up the street of the infantry quarters, as far as to the ice-house bastion, where two batteries had been placed to command the Mittelbronn hill. There we could see the road to Paris as far as to Petit Saint Jean, and even to Lixheim; but those great heaps of earth, called *cavaliers*, were covered with people; Baron Parmentier, his assistant Pipelingre, the old curate Leth, and many other men of note were there, in the midst of the crowd, looking on in silence. We had only to see their faces to know that something dreadful was happening.

From this height on the talus, we saw what was riveting everybody's attention. All our enemies, Austrians, Bavarians, Wurtemburgers, Russians, cavalry and infantry mixed together, were swarming around their intrenchments like ants, embracing each other, shaking hands, lifting their shakos on the points of their bayonets, waving branches of trees just beginning to turn green. Horsemen dashed across the plain, with their colbacs on the point of their swords, and rending the air with their shouts.

The telegraph was in operation on the hill of Saint Jean; Burguet pointed it out to me.

"If we understood those signals, Moses," said he, "we should know better what was going to happen to us in the next fortnight."

Some persons having turned round to listen to us, we went down again into the streets of the quarters, very thoughtfully.

The soldiers at the upper windows of the barracks were also looking out. Men and women in great numbers were collecting in the street.

We went through the crowd. In the street of the Capuchins, which was always deserted, Burguet, who was walking with his head down, exclaimed:

"So it is all over! What things have we seen in these last twenty-five years, Moses! What astonishing and terrible things! And it is all over!"

He took hold of my hand, and looked at me as if he were astonished at his own words; then he began to walk on.

"This winter campaign has been frightful to me," said he; "it has dragged along—dragged along—

and the thunderbolt did not come! But to-morrow, the day after to-morrow, what are we going to hear? Is the Emperor dead? How will that affect us? Will France still be France? What will they leave us? What will they take from us?"

Reflecting on these things, we came in front of our house. Then, as if suddenly wakened, Burguet said to me:

"Prudence, Moses! If the Emperor is not dead, the veterans will hold out till the last second. Remember that, and whoever they suspect will have everything to fear."

I thanked him, and went up, promising myself that I would follow his advice.

My wife and children were waiting breakfast for me, with the little basket of potatoes upon the table. We sat down, and I told them in a low voice what was to be seen from the top of the ramparts, and charged them to keep silent, for the danger was not over; the garrison might revolt and choose to defend itself, in spite of the officers; and those who mixed themselves in these matters, either for or against, even only in words, ran the risk of destruction without profit to any one.

They saw that I was right, and I had no need of saying more.

We were afraid that our sergeant would come,

and that we should be obliged to answer him, if he asked what we thought of these matters; but he did not come in till about eleven, when we had all been in bed for a long time.

The next day the news of the entrance of the allies to Paris was affixed to the church doors and the pillars of the market; it was never known by whom! M. de Vablerie, and three or four other emigrants, capable of such a deed, were spoken of at the time, but nothing was known with certainty.

The mounted guard tore down the placards, but unfortunately not before the soldiers and citizens had read them.

It was something so new, so incredible, after those ten years of war, when the Emperor had been everything, and the nation had been, so to speak, in the shadow; when not a man had dared to speak or write a word without permission; when men had had no other rights than those of paying, and giving their sons as conscripts,—it was such a great matter to think that the Emperor could have been conquered, that a man like myself in the midst of his family shook his head three or four times, before daring to breathe a single word.

So everybody kept quiet, notwithstanding the placards. The officials stayed at home, so as not to have to talk about it; the governor and council of defence did not stir; but the last recruits, in the hope of going home to their villages, embracing their families, and returning to their trades or farming, did not conceal their joy, as was very natural. The veterans, whose only trade and only means of living was war, were full of indignation! They did not believe a word of it; they declared that the reports were all false, that the Emperor had not lost a battle, and that the placards and the cannon-firing of the allies were only a stratagem to make us open the gates.

And from that time, Fritz, the men began to desert, not one at a time, but by sixes, by tens, by twenties. Whole posts filed off over the mountain with their arms and baggage. The veterans fired upon the deserters; they killed some of them, and were ordered to escort the conscripts who carried soup to the outposts. * * * * *

During this time, the flag of truce officers did nothing but come and go, one after another. All, Russian, Austrian, Bavarian, staff-officers stayed whole hours at the head-quarters, having, no doubt, important matters to discuss.

Our sergeant came to our room only for a moment in the evening, to complain of the desertions, and we were glad of it; Zeffen was still sick, Sorlé could not leave her, and I had to help Sâfel until the people went home.

The shop was always full of veterans; as soon as one set went away another came.

These old, gray-headed men swallowed down glass after glass of brandy; they paid by turns, and grew more and more down-hearted. They trembled with rage, and talked of nothing but treason, while they looked at you as if they would see through you.

Sometimes they would smile and say:

"I tell you! if it is necessary to blow up the fortress, it will go!"

Sâfel and I pretended not to understand; but you can imagine our agony; after having suffered all that we had, to be in danger of being blown up with those veterans!

That evening our sergeant repeated word for word what the others had said: "It was all nothing but lies and treason. The Emperor would put a stop to it by sweeping off this rabble!"

"Just wait! Just wait!" he exclaimed, as he smoked his pipe, with his teeth set. "It will all be cleared up soon! The thunderbolt is coming! And, this time, no pity, no mercy! All the villains will have to go then—all the traitors! The country will have to be cleansed for a hundred years! Never mind, Moses, we'll laugh!"

You may well suppose that we did not feel like laughing.

But the day when I was most anxious was the eighth of April, in the morning, when the decree of the Senate, deposing the Emperor, appeared.

Our shop was full of marine artillery-men and subalterns from the storehouses. We had just served them, when the secretary of the treasury, a short stout man, with full yellow cheeks, and the regulation cap over his ears, came in and called for a glass; he then took the decree from his pocket.

"Listen!" said he, as he began calmly to read it to the others.

It seems as if I could hear it now:

"Whereas, Napoleon Bonaparte has violated the compact which bound him to the French nation, by levying taxes otherwise than in virtue of the law, by unnecessarily adjourning the Legislative Body, by illegally making many decrees involving sentence of death, by annulling the authority of the ministers, the independence of the judiciary, the freedom of the press, etc.; Whereas, Napoleon has filled up the measure of the country's misfortunes, by his abuse of all the means of war committed to him, in men and money, and by refusing to treat on conditions which the national interest required him to accept; Whereas, the manifest wish of all the French demands an order of things, the first result of which shall be the re-establishment of general peace, and which shall also be the epoch of solemn reconciliation between all the States of the great European family, the Senate decrees: Napoleon Bonaparte has forfeited the throne; the right of succession is abolished in his family; the people and the army are released from the oath of allegiance to him."

He had scarcely begun to read when I thought: "If that goes on they will tear down my shop over my head."

In my fright, I even sent Säfel out hastily by the back door. But it all happened very differently from what I expected. These veterans despised the Senate; they shrugged their shoulders, and the one who read the decree sniffed at it, and threw it under the counter. "The Senate!" said he. "What is the Senate? A set of hangers-on, a set of sycophants that the Emperor has bribed, right and left, to keep saying to him—'*God bless you!*'"

"Yes, major," said another; "but they ought to be kicked out all the same."

"Bah! It is not worth the trouble," replied the sergeant-major· "a fortnight hence, when the Em peror is master again, they will come and lick his boots. Such men are necessary in a dynasty—men who lick your boots—it has a good effect!—especially old nobility, who are paid thirty or forty thousand francs a year. They will come back, and be quiet, and the Emperor will pardon them, especially since he cannot find others noble enough to fill their places."

And as they all went away after emptying their glasses, I thanked heaven for having given them such confidence in the Emperor.

This confidence lasted till about the eleventh or twelfth of April, when some officers, sent by the general commanding the fourth military division, came to say that the garrison of Metz recognized the Senate and followed its orders.

This was a terrible blow for our veterans. We saw, that evening, by our sergeant's face, that it was a death-blow to him. He looked ten years older, and you would have wept merely to see his face. Up to that time he had kept saying: "All these decrees, all these placards are acts of treason! The Emperor is down yonder with his army, all the while, and we are here to support him. Don't fear, Father Moses!"

But since the arrival of the officers from Metz, he had lost his confidence. He came into our room.

without speaking, and stood up, very pale, looking at us.

I thought: "But this man loves us. He has been kind to us. He gave us his fresh meat all through the blockade; he loved our little David; he fondled him on his knees. He loves Esdras too. He is a good, brave man, and here he is, so wretched!"

I wanted to comfort him, to tell him that he had friends, that we all loved him, that we would make sacrifices to help him, if he had to change his employment; yes, I thought of all this, but as I looked at him his grief seemed so terrible that I could not say a word.

He took two or three turns and stopped again, then suddenly went out. His sorrow was too great, he would not even speak of it.

At length, on the sixteenth of April, an armistice was concluded for burying the dead. The bridge of the German Gate was lowered, and large numbers of people went out and stayed till evening, to dig the ground a little with their spades, and try to bring back a few green things. Zeffen being all this time sick, we stayed at home.

That evening two new officers from Metz, sent as envoys, came in at night as the bridges were being raised. They galloped along the street to the headquarters. I saw them pass.

The arrival of these officers greatly excited the hopes and fears of every one; important measures were expected, and all night long we heard the sergeant walk to and fro in his room, get up, walk about, and lie down again, talking confusedly to himself.

The poor man felt that a dreadful blow was coming, and he had not a minute's rest. I heard him lamenting, and his sighs kept me from sleeping.

The next morning at ten the assembly was beat. The governor and the members of the council of defence went, in full dress, to the infantry quarters.

Everybody in the city was at the windows.

Our sergeant went down, and I followed him in a few minutes. The street was thronged with people. I made my way through the crowd; everybody kept his place in it, trying to move on.

When I came in front of the barracks, the companies had just formed in a circle; the quartermasters in the midst were reading in a loud voice the order of the day; it was the abdication of the Emperor, the disbanding of the recruits of 1813 and 1814, the recognition of Louis XVIII., the order to set up the white flag and change the cockade!

Not a murmur was heard from the ranks; all was quiet, terrible, frightful! Those old soldiers, their teeth set, their moustaches shaking, their brows scowling fiercely, presenting arms in silence; the voices of the quarter-masters stopping now and then as if choking; the staff-officers of the place, at a distance under the arch, sullen, with their eyes on the ground; the eager attention of all that crowd of men, women, and children, through the whole length of the street, leaning forward on tip-toe, with open mouths and listening ears; all this, Fritz, would have made you tremble.

I was on cooper Schweyer's steps, where I could see everything and hear every word.

So long as the order of the day was read, nobody stirred; but at the command:—Break ranks! a terrible cry arose from all directions; tumult, confusion, fury burst forth at once.

People did not know what they were doing. The conscripts ran in files to the postern gates, the old soldiers stood a moment, as if rooted to the spot, then their rage broke forth; one tore off his epaulettes, another dashed his musket with both hands against the pavement; some officers doubled up their sabres and swords, which snapped apart with a crash.

The governor tried to speak; he tried to form the ranks again, but nobody heard him; the new recruits were already in all the rooms at the barracks, making up their bundles to start on their journey;

the old ones were going to the right and left, as if they were drunk or mad.

I saw some of these old soldiers stop in a corner lean their heads against the wall, and weep bitterly.

At last all were dispersed, and protracted cries reached from the barracks to the square, incessant cries, which rose and fell like sighs.

Some low, despairing shouts of "*Vive l'Empereur!*" but not a single shout of "*Vive le Roi!*"

For my part, I ran home to tell about it all; I had scarcely gone up, when the sergeant came also, with his musket on his shoulder. We should have liked to congratulate each other on the ending of the blockade, but on seeing the sergeant standing at the door, we were chilled to the bones, and our attention was fixed upon him.

"Ah, well!" said he, placing the butt-end of his musket upon the floor, "it is all ended!"

And for a moment he said no more.

Then he stammered out: "This is the shabbiest piece of business in the world—the recruits are disbanded—they are leaving—France remains, bound hand and foot, in the grip of the kaiserlicks! Ah! the rascals! the rascals!"

"Yes, sergeant," I replied with emotion, seeing that his thoughts must be diverted: "now we are going to have peace, sergeant! You have a sister left in the Jura, you will go to her——"

"Oh!" he exclaimed, lifting his hand, "my poor sister!"

This came like a sob; but he quickly recovered himself, and went and placed his musket in the corner by the door.

He sat down at the table with us for a moment, and took up little Säfel, drawing him to him and caressing his cheeks. Then he wanted to hold Esdras also. We looked on in silence.

"I am going to leave you, Father Moses," said he, "I am going to pack my bag. Thunder and lightning! I am sorry to leave you!"

"And we are sorry, too, sergeant," said Sorlé, mournfully; "but if you will live with us——"

"It is impossible!"

"Then you remain in the service?"

"Service of whom—of what?" said he; "of Louis XVIII.? No! no! I know no one but my General —but that makes it hard to go—when a man has done his duty——"

He started up, and shouted in a piercing voice: "*Vive l'Empereur!*"

We trembled, we did not know why.

I reached out my hand to him, and rose; we embraced each other like brothers.

"Good-by, Father Moses," said he, "good-by for a long while."

"You are going at once, then?"

"Yes!"

"You know, sergeant, that you will always have friends here. You will come and see us. If you need anything——"

"Yes, yes, I know it. You are true friends— excellent people!"

He shook my hand vehemently.

Then he took up his musket, and we were all following him, expressing our good wishes, when he turned, with tears in his eyes, and embraced my wife, saying:

"I must embrace you, too; there is no harm in it, is there, Madame Sorlé?"

"Oh, no!" said she, "you are one of the family, and I will embrace Zeffen for you!"

He went out at once, exclaiming in a hoarse voice, "Good-by! Farewell!"

I saw him go into his room at the end of the little passage.

Twenty-five years of service, eight wounds, and no bread in his old age! My heart bled at the thought of it.

About a quarter of an hour after, the sergeant came down with his musket. Meeting Sâfel or the stairs, he said to him, "Stay, that is for your father!"

It was the portrait of the landwehr's wife and children. Sâfel brought it to me at once. I took the poor devil's gift, and looked at it for a long time, very sadly; then I shut it up in the closet with the letter.

It was noon, and, as the gates were about to be opened, and abundance of provisions were to come, we sat down before a large piece of boiled beef, with a dish of potatoes, and opened a good bottle of wine.

We were still eating when we heard shouts in the street. Sâfel got up to look out.

"A wounded soldier that they are carrying to the hospital!" said he.

Then he exclaimed, "It is our sergeant!"

A horrible thought ran through my mind. "Keep still!" I said to Sorlé, who was getting up, and I went down alone.

Four marine gunners were carrying the litter by on their shoulders; children were running behind.

At the first glance I recognized the sergeant; his face perfectly white and his breast covered with blood. He did not move. The poor fellow had gone from our house to the bastion behind the arsenal, to shoot himself through the heart.

I went up so overwhelmed, so sad and sorrowful, that I could scarcely stand.

Sorlé was waiting for me in great agitation.

"Our poor sergeant has killed himself," said I; "may God forgive him!"

And, sitting down, I could not help bursting into tears!

XXL

It is said with truth that misfortunes never come singly; one brings another in its train. The death of our good sergeant was, however, the last.

That same day the enemy withdrew his outposts to six hundred yards from the city, the white flag was raised on the church, and the gates were opened.

Now, Fritz, you know about our blockade. Should I tell you, in addition, about Baruch's coming, of Zeffen's cries, and the groanings of us all, when we had to say to the good man: "Our little David is dead—thou wilt never see him again!"

No, it is enough! If we were to speak of all the miseries of war, and all their consequences in after years, there would be no end!

I would rather tell you of my sons Itzig and Frômel, and of my Sâfel, who has gone to join them in America.

If I should tell you of all the wealth they have acquired in that great country of freemen, of the lands they have bought, the money they have laid up, the number of grandchildren they have given me, and of all the blessings they have heaped upon Sorlé and myself, you would be full of astonishment and admiration.

They have never allowed me to want for anything. The greatest pleasure I can give them is to wish for something; each of them wants to send it to me! They do not forget that by my prudent foresight I saved them from the war.

I love them all alike, Fritz, and I say of them, like Jacob:

"May the God of Abraham and Isaac, our fathers, the God which fed me all my life long unto this day, bless the lads; let them grow into a multitude in the midst of the earth, and their seed become a multitude of nations!"

www.ingramcontent.com/pod-product-compliance
Lightning Source LLC
Chambersburg PA
CBHW030811230426
43667CB00008B/1159